FINDING·JESUS *in* HIS PRAYERS

To Senford

with blessings,

Steve

Shoemaker

FINDING JESUS *in* HIS PRAYERS

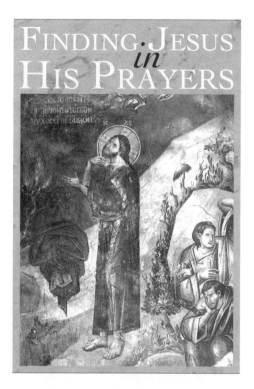

H. STEPHEN SHOEMAKER

Abingdon Press
Nashville

FINDING JESUS IN HIS PRAYERS

Copyright © 2004 by H. Stephen Shoemaker

Library of Congress Cataloging-in-Publication Data

Shoemaker, H. Stephen, 1948-
    Finding Jesus in his prayers/ H. Stephen Shoemaker.
        p. cm.
    Includes bibliographical references.
    ISBN 0-687-35253-3 (binding: adhesive, pbk. : alk. paper)
    1. Jesus Christ—Prayers.   2. Prayer—Christianity.   I. Title.

BV229.S54 2004
232.9'5—dc22
                                                                        2004010912

04 05 06 07 08 09 10 11 12 13 — 10 9 8 7 6 5 4 3 2 1

MANUFACTURED IN THE UNITED STATES OF AMERICA

To Myers Park Baptist Church, Charlotte, North Carolina, with whom I am seeking to answer Jesus' call.

The kingdom of God is near! Turn ... and believe the good news. —Mark 1:15 AT

Contents

Preface

This book was begun with the purpose of filling in a gap: two few books on prayer or about Jesus took serious enough notice of how Jesus prayed. But it soon took on a more urgent purpose.

I began this book in the summer of 2001, weeks before the September 11 tragedy. No one could have imagined the savagery of that day. Nor could most have imagined that religion would reenter the world of global politics after its banishment to the margin of life in the modern period.

It seems particularly important for people in all the world's religions to rediscover their spiritual roots, which will help them salt the world with peace rather than leave their religions vulnerable to the uses of political and ideological power.

I found myself praying and repraying the prayers of Jesus in the aftermath of September 11. Two and one-half years later, the issues seem no less crucial. In the days of that fall, we heard various uses of "prayer" in public pronouncements: From presidents, terrorists, religious leaders, and politicians.

What seems urgently clear is that how we pray reflects the *character* of the God in whom we believe and to whom we pray. What kind of God do we pray to? What are we asking this God to do? What is the purpose of our praying?

What seems now more urgently clear is that how we pray can mean life and death to people. It seems critically important, then, for us to ask again the disciples' question, "Lord, teach us how to pray."

I wish to thank my congregation, Myers Park Baptist Church, a people of God seeking to be Christian and to learn a deeper

ecumenism in the world where religion can contribute to our tin-
derbox world. Flannery O'Connor pegged the Bible Belt South as
a region less "Christ-centered" as "Christ-haunted." The congregation I have been given as a community of faith is a congregation haunted by Jesus' vision of the kingdom and is on a quest to
find and follow the Jesus of the Gospels. To them I dedicate this
book.

I thank two friends and colleagues, Pat Hice, my dedicated
administrative assistant, and Velma Stevens, editor-friend, who
have helped get these words to my publisher and to you, the
reader. Finally, I thank Abingdon Press for reading these words
sent to them and wanting to publish them.

H. Stephen Shoemaker
Holy Week, 2004

The Prayers of Jesus and the Story of Jesus

The Prayers of Jesus

THE DAILY PRAYER, OR LORD'S PRAYER

Matthew 6:9-13; parallel Luke 11:2-4

> Our *Abba* in heaven,
> hallowed be your name.
> Your kingdom come.
> Your will be done on earth as in heaven.
> Give us today our daily bread.
> Forgive us our sins
> as we forgive those who sin against us.
> Save us in the time of trial
> and deliver us from evil.
> For yours is the kingdom
> and the power and the glory
> now and forever.
> Amen.

THE PRAYER OF THANKSGIVING AMID LIFE'S REVERSALS

Matthew 11:25-26 NRSV, adapted

> I thank you, *Abba*,
> Lord of heaven and earth,
> that you have hidden these things
> from the wise and learned
> and revealed them to little ones;
> yes, *Abba*, for such was your gracious will.

THE GETHSEMANE PRAYER

Mark 14:36 NRSV, adapted

> *Abba*, all things are possible to you;
> remove this cup from me;
> yet, not what I want, but what you want.

THE PRAYERS FROM THE CROSS

> *Abba*, forgive them; for they know not what they do. (Luke 23:34 RSV, adapted)

> "Eli, Eli, lama sabach-tha-ni?" that is, "My God, my God, why hast thou forsaken me?" (Matthew 27:46)

> *Abba*, into thy hands I commit my spirit! (Luke 23:46 RSV, adapted)

PRAYERS FROM JOHN'S GOSPEL

Jesus' prayer at Lazarus's tomb before Lazarus is raised from the dead:

> *Abba*, I thank you that you have heard me.
> I know that you always hear me.
> But I have said this because of the crowd standing here,
> that they may believe that you sent me. (John 11:41-2
> NRSV, adapted)

John's parallel to the Gethsemane prayer:

> Now my soul is troubled.
> And what shall I say,
> "*Abba*, save me from this hour"?
> No, for this purpose I have come to this hour.
> *Abba*, glorify your name. (John 12:27 RSV, adapted)

The key verse of the "high priestly prayer":

> Holy *Abba*, keep them in your name
> which you have given to me,
> that they may be one,
> even as we are one. (John 17:11*b* RSV, adapted)

The Story of Jesus

Each of the four Gospels provides its own story or portrait of Jesus. Here is my working summary of what they tell us. (This summary is, of course, outrageously incomplete and will always be open to revision.)

A son was born to Mary (*Miriam*), a young Jewish maiden. She and her betrothed, a carpenter from Nazareth named Joseph (*Yosef*), named the child Jesus or *Yeshua*, a form of the Hebrew name Joshua. They were Galilean commoners with no special social or religious standing.

About the age of thirty this man named Jesus began his public ministry by being washed by John the Baptizer in the Jordan River. A one-man reform movement within Judaism, John offered a way of radical repentance and purification that did not depend upon the temple sacrifice system. You could be washed for free, the only requirement being a heart ready to turn and be changed by God. As Jesus rose from the Jordan's waters, the Spirit of God descended like a dove and a voice from heaven said, "You are my son, the beloved; in you I am well pleased."

Full of the Spirit, anointed with sonship, Jesus set out on his own reform movement. He called disciples to follow him: the Twelve, a symbolic circle of men, and a larger group of disciples that surprisingly included women. He healed and taught. He preached the kingdom of God, not as some distant hope but as a compelling, immediate, urgent, and gracious opportunity. His ministry challenged the religious and political structures, dominated as they were by holiness maps and purity codes,[1] with his offer of the free grace of God and his call to live in the presence of the Spirit. As had Hebrew prophets of old, he challenged social structures of greed, injustice, and exploitation.

His ready miracles and flowing forgiveness undermined an elaborate and increasingly oppressive system of temple sacrifice and religious purification. His table fellowship, open to all, embodied the graciousness of the kingdom he preached. He ate with saint and sinner, clean and unclean alike, with outcasts, prostitutes, tax collectors, and those outside the law of Moses. Women were given equal status with men; Gentiles were being healed; crowds began to form and follow wherever he went; the kingdom was coming to all.

Opposition started early. His hometown congregation heard an early sermon and were so enraged they tried to throw him off a cliff. Official religious leaders were threatened, not only because he undermined the religious status quo but also because his growing popularity threatened the fragile political peace. The Roman overlords might smell insurrection at work and come down with full military fury upon Israel.

At some point in his ministry, Jesus began to suspect his death was inevitable. He also began to envision that his death might play a vital role in God's redemption of the world and in the coming of God's kingdom. He would become God's "suffering servant," one who had come to give his life "as a ransom for many" (Mark 10:45).

Jesus foretold his death three times and "set his face" to go to Jerusalem, where he anticipated it would happen. An entrance into Jerusalem on a donkey and the prophetic act of "cleansing" the Temple brought things to a head. He was arrested, tried in both religious and political courts, and sentenced to death by the Roman authorities as an insurrectionist, a so-called King of the Jews. He died the most humiliating of deaths, reserved for the worst of offenders: death by Roman crucifixion.

This happened on a Friday during the Jewish Passover. On the following Sunday morning an empty tomb was discovered, and a risen Jesus began to appear in a "resurrection body" to his closest disciples and friends, most of whom had deserted him. His return to them was marked by forgiveness and a new call to follow him. As God had sent ("apostled") Jesus, Jesus was now sending, "apostling," his followers to be heralds of the kingdom, to be the ongoing incarnation of Christ, Jesus' own hands and feet in the world. Filled with the Spirit of God, fired by the experiences with the risen Jesus, the Christian movement began.

INTRODUCTION

Setting the Stage

O ur present day has witnessed the rebirth of interest in spirituality and a renewed quest for the historical Jesus. This book's purpose is to join the two by taking seriously the way Jesus prayed as an entryway into who Jesus was. Our quest is to find Jesus in his prayers, and in finding him there, learn better how to follow in his way.

Jesus was a Jewish prophet seeking to renew his beloved faith. He saw himself sent by God to inaugurate the new age of the kingdom of God. He was a social and religious reformer who was executed by the powers that be, and who saw his approaching death as the sacrifice of God's suffering servant that God would use for the redemption of the world. But all of this had an experiential core, a spiritual antecedent: his relationship with God whom he called *Abba*.[1] Behind, beneath it all was what has been called his *"Abba*-experience." His prayers reveal the spiritual core of his life with God and help us better understand his spiritual vision and mission. So we believe, so we pray. Prayer is the basic theology. Do you want to know what a person believes and does not believe? Watch how they pray. So it is with Jesus.

Prayer is "primary speech,"[2] the elemental offering to God of all we are, all our desires, fears, hopes, rages, and loves. Prayer involves the utterable and the unutterable, words and all within us too deep for words.

Prayer is also speech shaped by God's presence within us, where "deep calls unto deep." It is a comingling of our own spirit, wind, breath with God's spirit, wind, breath. (The ancient Hebrew word for Spirit, *ruach*, means all three.) We are being shaped by what we pray even if we are unaware of what is being changed. Kathleen Norris, a poet and Christian lay theologian, says that when we pray we say, "I mean these words even if I don't know what I mean."[3]

The great spiritual traditions of the world include in their teachings the practice of prayer. Prayer is the elemental theology of a people passed along in the practice. It shapes their spiritual identity. Jesus' disciples were right to ask, "Lord, teach us to pray."

New Testament scholar E. F. Scott reminded us that Jesus gave his followers not a creed but a prayer.[4] We might quibble and say that prayer is our primal creed, our most elemental *credo*, "I believe." But Scott is right. And Jesus gave us not one prayer, but nine. Together these prayers help us know Jesus' spiritual core. Together they may help form ours.

Recently in America a book called *The Prayer of Jabez* has become enormously popular.[5] It is based on a short four-line prayer of a once mentioned figure in the Hebrew Scriptures. It is too obscure a prayer to be the basis of one's spirituality, and it leaves too much room for one to read one's own spiritual inclinations between the lines. In our American cultural context, our spiritual inclinations lean to the preoccupation with the self and its needs rather than to the mystery of God and the urgent needs of humanity. Jesus' prayers are a corrective to the ways our culture wants to pray—and to the ways the American church prefers to pray. Perhaps if we let Jesus' prayers form our way of praying there would come a new reformation, a church closer to the heart of God and more redemptively engaged with God's world.

I offer in this book the nine prayers placed on Jesus' lips in the four New Testament Gospels.[6] They reveal the spiritual life of Jesus and can become a guide to our own spiritual life. As you read these pages, I hope you will hear the sound of Jesus praying. If we pray these prayers along with Jesus we will not be unchanged. The same Spirit that called these prayers forth in Jesus will prompt them in us and shape us who pray them now. At least this is my hope. When I pray them, I find myself saner, more centered, less neurotic, less apt to live out of what I call the "false self," more apt to live out of what I experience as my true self.

So, again, here are the nine prayers of Jesus.

1. "The Daily Prayer," or "Lord's Prayer," found in Matthew 6:9-13 with its parallel in Luke 11:2-4, the prayer of the kingdom of God Jesus taught his disciples to pray:

> Our *Abba* in heaven,[7]
> hallowed be your name.
> Your kingdom come.
> Your will be done on earth as in heaven.
> Give us today our daily bread.
> Forgive us our sins
> as we forgive those who sin against us.
> Save us in the time of trial
> and deliver us from evil.
> For yours is the kingdom
> and the power and the glory
> now and forever.
> Amen.[8]

2. "The Prayer of Thanksgiving amid Life's Reversals," found in Matthew 11:25-26 (NRSV, adapted), a prayer that is a window open to the spirituality of Jesus:

> I thank you, *Abba*,
> Lord of heaven and earth,
> that you have hidden these things
> from the wise and learned
> and revealed them to little ones;
> yes, *Abba*, for such was your gracious will.

3. "The Gethsemane Prayer," prayed the night before his public execution, found in Mark 14:36 (NRSV, adapted), with parallel versions in Matthew 26:39 and Luke 22:42:

Abba, all things are possible to you;
remove this cup from me;
yet, not what I want, but what you want.

4-6. "The Prayers from the Cross," three of the "seven last words" of Jesus:

Abba, forgive them; for they know not what they do. (Luke 23:34 RSV, adapted)

"Eli, Eli, lama sabach-tha-ni?" that is, "My God, my God, why hast thou forsaken me?" (Matthew 27:46)

Abba, into thy hands I commit my spirit! (Luke 23:46 RSV, adapted)

7-9. "Prayers from John's Gospel." There are three. The first is Jesus' prayer at Lazarus's tomb before Lazarus is raised from the dead:

Abba, I thank you that you have heard me.
I know that you always hear me.
But I have said this because of the crowd standing here,
that they may believe that you sent me. (John 11:41-42 NRSV, adapted)

The second is John's parallel to the Gethsemane prayer found in the other Gospels:

Now my soul is troubled.
And what shall I say,
"*Abba*, save me from this hour"?
No, for this purpose I have come to this hour.
Abba, glorify your name. (John 12:27 RSV, adapted)

The last is the key verse of the "high priestly prayer" that encompasses all of chapter 17:

> Holy *Abba*, keep them in your name
> which you have given to me,
> that they may be one,
> even as we are one. (John 17:11*b* RSV, adapted)

ABBA AND THE WORDS OF THE HISTORICAL JESUS

You have by now noted that in my translation of Jesus' prayers I have substituted the Aramaic word *Abba* for the English word "father." In eight of the nine prayers, all except Jesus' cry of dereliction, "Eli, Eli . . . ," which is a quote of Psalm 22:1, Jesus addressed God as "father." The Greek word used in the Gospels was "pater." In Mark's Gethsemane prayer we see both the Aramaic *Abba* and the Greek "pater" used: "*Abba, ho pater*" or "*Abba*, the father" (Mark 14:36).

I work with the assumption of the correctness of Joachim Jeremias—that behind every "pater" in the Gospels there is the echo of Jesus' Aramaic name for God, *Abba*. Therefore, I have chosen to translate the Greek word backward into *Abba* rather than forward into the English word "father."

I have chosen this translation for two reasons. The first is to emphasize the centrality of the "*Abba*-experience" to Jesus' spiritual life and of the *Abba* as his most characteristic address to God in prayer.

The second reason is to force us back into the strange and different world of Jesus and his mode of speaking. We can think of two major translation strategies. One is to make the original language as easy as possible for us to understand in our most accustomed way of speaking and understanding. The other strategy is to force us into the strangeness of the ancient language and its world. The first way helps the text enter our linguistic world. The second way forces us into the foreignness of the text's linguistic world. Sometimes in the teaching enterprise we need to make the strange familiar; other times we need to make the familiar strange. Both are important strategies.

I use the word *Abba* to force us into a world different from our own because we presume too much familiarity with Jesus and his world. To use "father" leads us to assume too quickly what the name means. Using *Abba* slows us down and makes us ask, *Why did Jesus use* Abba *and what did it mean?* Chapter 2 will take up this question.

A second question is, *Did Jesus actually pray all these prayers?* I describe the prayers as "the nine prayers placed on Jesus' lips." These prayers are not direct quotations as we might expect from modern sources. The nine prayers represent one of three levels of historical remembrance: (1) accurate historical memory of Jesus' actual words, passed along in oral transmission then translated into Greek; (2) a capturing of the ideas of Jesus in paraphrased form; or (3) the words the early church heard the Living Christ speaking to them through the Spirit, words that adapted and extended the meaning of Jesus' message to the situation of the church community living thirty to seventy years after Jesus' life.

Critical New Testament scholarship seeks to differentiate between these layers. The most radical of scholars see the later layer as a deliberate distortion of Jesus' words. The Jesus Seminar has taken up the quest to discern those words that are most likely to be Jesus' words and which words are more likely to be the early church's words.

I find historical, critical scholarship to be helpful, especially as it helps us avoid misunderstandings of Jesus that may arise from the later layers of the Gospel writings. For example, there is a growing anti-Jewish tone in the later Gospels that reflects not the historical Jesus, but the increasing hostility between the synagogue and the Jewish Christian church in the last half of the first century.

My own presuppositions used in this study are that the nine prayers of Jesus—wherever they fall in the mix of the three layers of historical tradition delineated above—are a reliable guide to the spirit and message of the historical Jesus and to his spirit that is yet today teaching us how to pray.

The purpose and posture of this study is less that of a scientist dissecting a corpse or an archeologist uncovering the layers of history and more of a believer's conversation with Jesus and his interpreters that helps us follow in the way of the kingdom of God embodied in Jesus' life, death, and resurrection.

Let's listen in as we hear Jesus praying, inquire what these prayers may have meant to him and to his world, and consider what they would mean to us if we were to pray them.

A caution: As I draw a portrait of Jesus from his prayers, the portrait will inevitably be in some measure a self-portrait. My prayer is that my face does not obscure our view of him who is to me "surprise of Mercy, outgoing Gladness, Rescue, Healing and Life," as he was described by my beloved teacher George Buttrick.[9]

Walter Brueggemann, the prophetic and incisive biblical scholar, cautions modern enlightened readers not to rush too quickly to the historical questions, however important they are. If we ask too soon "what happened?" or "what could have happened?" we rob the text of its capacity to speak its alternative voice to us and our culture. We should be as those who "stand before" the text listening for God's word in it rather than as those who stand over the text as its judges.[10]

The anecdote is told of a debate between the famous New Testament scholar Rudolf Bultmann, who championed his method of "demythologizing" the New Testament, and a young New Testament scholar from Yale, Paul Minear. At one point Minear said, "The major difference, Mr. Bultmann, is clear. Your concern is that we demythologize the New Testament. Mine is that we allow the New Testament to demythologize us."[11]

As we search out the meaning of Jesus' prayers, can we leave some room for his prayers to search us out? I think as we do those prayers will help us live with deeper truthfulness and grace.

CHAPTER 1

Jesus and Prayer

J esus' way of praying is given to us not only in the words of his prayers, but also in his habits of prayer and his teaching about prayer. This first chapter will examine the habit of prayer Jesus inherited from his Jewish faith and his teachings about prayer that were both continuous and discontinuous with his tradition. There is both something ancient and something new in Jesus' way of praying.

(1) Jesus participated in the daily rhythm of Jewish prayers: every morning, afternoon, and evening. Morning and afternoon prayers always included the *Shema*:

> Hear, O Israel:
> The Lord is our God,
> The Lord is one. (Deuteronomy 6:4 AT)

The afternoon prayer featured the *Tephillah*, whose first benediction blesses Yahweh as God of Abraham, Isaac, and Jacob, "most high God and Master of heaven and earth ... our shield."[1] The early church adopted this rhythm of prayer by praying the Lord's Prayer three times a day.[2] They would not have likely carried this rhythm on had not Jesus been faithful in this daily discipline of prayer.

(2) Jesus prayed the Hebrew blessings before and after meals. Before the meal he prayed:

> Blessed be thou, Lord our God, king of the world
> Who makest bread to come forth from the earth.[3]

After the meal was a three-part thanksgiving, the *Birkat ha-mazon*, which combined a prayer for mercy upon Israel with a prayer of thanksgiving for nourishment and for the land.[4]

(3) Jesus prayed the prayers of the weekly Shabbat service in the synagogue, "as his custom was" (Luke 4:16), which included the *Shema*, the *Tephillah*, and concluded with the *Kaddish*, which formed the background of Jesus' "Lord's Prayer":

> May his great name be magnified and sanctified
> in the world that he created according to his good pleasure!
> May he make his reign prevail
> during your life and during your days,
> and during the life of the entire house of Israel
> at this very moment and very soon.
>   And let them say: Amen!
>
> May the name of the Lord—blessed be he!—
> be blessed, praised, glorified, extolled,
> exalted, honored, magnified, and hymned!
> It is above and beyond
> any blessing, hymn, praise, consolation
> that men utter in this world.
>   And let them say: Amen![5]

(4) Jesus engaged in extemporaneous and private prayer. To describe his prayer life from within Israel's traditional prayers does not tell us enough. The Gospels portray him as one who spent hours, even whole nights, in solitary prayer:

> And in the morning, a great while
> before day, he rose and went out
> to a lonely place, and there he prayed. (Mark 1:35)
>
> And after he had taken leave of them,
> he went into the hills to pray. (Mark 6:46)

Especially before important decisions, he went aside for concentrated prayer:

> In these days he went out into the hills to pray;
> and all night he continued in prayer to God.
> And when it was day, he called his
> disciples. (Luke 6:12)

He also taught his disciples to observe a rhythm of action and prayer:

> The apostles returned to Jesus,
> and told them all that they had done
> and taught. And he said to them,
> "Come away by yourselves to a
> lonely place, and rest a while." (Mark 6:30-31)

(5) Jesus prayed prayers of blessing and intercession. He prayed for children and, laying his hands on them, blessed them (Mark 10:16). He prayed for his friends (John 17), for Jerusalem, and for his nation, Israel (Luke 19:41-42).

For Jesus, prayer was at times a spiritual combat with the forces of evil in the world. These are no wimpy prayers, but a call to arms: "Watch and pray, lest you enter into temptation" (Matthew 26:41 NKJV). Once Jesus' disciples came back discouraged because their spiritual power was not sufficient to drive out certain evil spirits. Jesus replied, "This kind cannot be driven out by anything but prayer" (Mark 9:29).

In Luke 22:31 Jesus describes his prayer for Peter in face of Peter's spiritual testing:

> Simon, Simon, behold, Satan demanded to have you, that he might sift you like wheat, but I have prayed for you that your faith may not fail; and when you have turned again, strengthen your brethren.

There is little doubt that Jesus saw prayer as a way of garnering the power of God in face of the power of evil.

We also learn of Jesus' way of prayer by his teaching about prayer. It was one of the things spiritual masters taught their disciples. So Jesus' disciples asked, "Lord, teach us to pray" (Luke 11:1). In answer Jesus taught at least these three things:

1. No show-offy prayers
2. No long-winded prayers
3. No embarrassed prayers

First, no show-offy prayers. In Matthew 6:1, 5 he warns against parading your prayers in public:

> Beware of practicing your piety before [others] in order to be seen by them.... And when you pray, you must not be like the hypocrites; for they love to stand and pray in the synagogues and at the street corners, that they may be seen by [others].

Jesus does not here forbid public prayer—he himself prayed publicly—but rather the kind of prayer we pray in order to be seen by others. He calls those who do so "hypocrites," which literally means, "play actors."

It is important to remember who it is to whom we pray. No one else matters. The anecdote is told about Bill Moyers when he was press secretary for President Lyndon B. Johnson. Johnson asked him to pray at some state dinner. Mid-prayer Johnson interrupted and said, "Speak up, Bill, I can't hear you." Moyers replied, "Mr. President, you're not the one I'm speaking to." So, Jesus says, no show-offy prayers designed for the admiration of others.

Second, prayers need not go on and on:

> And in praying do not heap up empty phrases as the Gentiles do; for they think that they will be heard for their many words. Do not be like them, for your Father knows what you need before you ask him. (Matthew 6:7-8)

Jesus is not forbidding all repetitive prayer, but rather the kind of praying that believes that it can, by its way of praying, earn

God's favor or wear God down until God finally listens. Jesus is saying, God's favor is already with you, God's ear is already inclined. No need to go on and on. God is your *Abba* who already knows your need and is coming to help.

Jesus' own practice of long solitary prayer suggests there is a place for repetitive and contemplative prayer. Such prayer is appropriate as a way of communing with God, of being in the presence of God. But this kind of prayer is very different from long prayers designed to curry favor with the Divine.

Third, Jesus says we need never be ashamed or embarrassed about coming to God for help.

In Luke 11, Jesus tells a parable about a man in a predicament. Someone has come to his house late at night and asked to stay. The sacred rules of hospitality of that time were that you always provided shelter when asked, and supplied a meal as well. Such rules were life-saving courtesies in the first-century world. The host is terribly embarrassed because he has nothing to give the guest to eat. So he goes to a friend's house at midnight. The door is shut, meaning everyone is in bed and the children are asleep—probably all in the same main room of the house. You know how hard it is to get children to go back to sleep once they have finally settled down! The man answers from within: "Do not bother me; the door is now shut, and my children are with me in bed" (Luke 11:7).

Jesus says, "Though he will not get up and give him anything because he is his friend, yet because of the man's *shamelessness*, he will get up and give him whatever he needs" (Luke 11:8, adapted).

The Greek word *anaideia* is often translated "importunity" or "persistence," and indeed Jesus taught us to be persistent in prayer. We are to pray and keep on praying, not as those who believe that we will finally wear God down, but because our praying is a sign of hope in the God who will make good on divine promises. But here, in this parable, I think we should translate *anaideia* "shamelessness," as it most often is translated in ancient literature.[6] And the meaning? God always wants to hear our voice. It doesn't matter how long it has been since we prayed, or what a mess we've made of our lives. God is ready to listen and to come to our aid. Don't let the feeling of shame keep you from approaching God in prayer.

Then Jesus adds to the teaching:

> If you then, who are evil, know how to give good gifts to
> your children, how much more will the heavenly Father give
> the Holy Spirit to those who ask him! (Luke 11:13 NRSV)

Our God is a "how much more" God, a God beyond our human
capacities to love and to give, so no ashamed prayer, no embarrassed prayer.

I heard of a businessmen's breakfast. As all the men were seated,
one last man rushed in at the last moment and sat down.
Naturally, they asked *him* to return thanks. After a long pause, he
began, "Lord, I know you're as surprised about this as I am."

Go boldly, unashamed before God. Bang on the door in the
middle of the night. It's okay. It doesn't matter if God hasn't heard
your voice for awhile. Nothing matters except that *you* matter to
God.

Joachim Jeremias, one of the great New Testament scholars of
our time, says: "Jesus appeared in this world with a new prayer."[7]
This new prayer, or new way of praying, begins with the word
Abba, the tenderest and most intimate address imaginable for
God. Our every prayer, our every word, our every breath matters
to this God. To this new prayer we now turn.

CHAPTER 2

The Lord's Prayer, Part 1

THE TEXTS OF THE LORD'S PRAYER: OR WHY DO SOME SAY "DEBTS," OTHERS "TRESPASSES," AND OTHERS "SINS"?

Matthew 6:9-13	Luke 11:2-4
9. Our Father who art in heaven, Hallowed be thy name.	2. Father, hallowed be thy name.
10. Thy kingdom come,	Thy kingdom come.
Thy will be done, On earth as it is in heaven.	

11. Give us this day
    our daily bread;

3. Give us each
   day our daily
   bread;

12. And forgive us our
    debts,
    As we also have
    forgiven our
    debtors;

4. and forgive us
   our sins,
   for we ourselves
   forgive every
   one who is
   indebted to us;

13. And lead us not
    into temptation,
    But deliver us from evil.
    [For thine is the kingdom
    and the power and the glory,
    forever. Amen.]

and lead us not
into temptation.

These two versions were written forty to sixty years after Jesus' death. The variations are due to the years of transmission in oral and pamphlet form. The variety of the words, "debts," "trespasses," and "sins," in the petition "Forgive us our debts" is due to the use of three different Greek words in the Matthew and Luke texts.

In Matthew 6:12, the Greek text says: "Forgive us our debts *(opheilemata)* as we forgive our debtors." This word may be closest to the Aramaic word Jesus most likely used, *hoba.* "Debts" was an Aramaic metaphor for sin that emphasized the debt that sin causes in relationship, a debt that cannot be repaid, only forgiven. But Jesus might also have used this word to voice the kingdom's call for us to forgive each other our financial debtors as well because indebtedness was so wrapped up in the exploitative economic conditions of his day.[1] This economic dimension of forgiveness was part of the Jewish tradition of the Jubilee year every forty-nine years when all debts were to be forgiven.[2]

In Matthew 6:14, in an explanatory teaching following the prayer, we see a second word appear:

> For if you forgive [others] their tres-passes *(paraptomata)*, your heavenly Father also will forgive you.

Paraptomata was a more general word for sin. When William Tyndale embarked upon his monumental and formative English translation of the Bible in 1526, the first in the English language, he translated both Greek words in verses 12 and 14 as "trespasses" because he thought it better communicated the general sense of sin.

The 1548 *Book of Common Prayer* used his translation, so Anglicans have most regularly prayed, "Forgive us our trespasses as we forgive those who trespass against us."

The King James Version of 1611, following the other pioneering English translation by Miles Coverdale (1535), used the more accurate word "debts": "Forgive us our debts as we forgive our debtors." So, many English Protestants other than Anglicans use the word "debts."

If that were not complicated enough, Luke's version used a third Greek word for sin, *hamartias,* another general word for sin; so it is often translated "Forgive us our *sins.*" Luke wanted to use a word for sin that was more generally used for sin in the Greek-speaking world. But he had a historian's knack for preservation so he retained the more Jewish notion of sin as "debts" in the second phrase: "for we forgive everyone who is indebted *[opheilonti]* to us." Luke both translates and preserves. He is like a man restoring a historic house who in some places leaves evidence of the original.

The doxology, "For thine is the kingdom and the power and the glory, forever. Amen," is not found in the earliest and best manuscripts. But it is a thoroughly Jewish way of praying to end a prayer with a doxology. (See 1 Chronicles 29:10-11.) Doxologies were thought to seal a prayer. So while Jesus may or may not have used the doxology, the early church soon used it as part of the prayer. [3]

From the first century on, the church began to pray the prayer as part of daily prayers and weekly worship. In the process they used various forms of the two versions. For example, Roman Catholics, following Luke and the earliest manuscripts, omit the doxology. For the purpose of this study I will use my adaptation of the ecumenical text from the *United Methodist Hymnal* (Nashville: United Methodist Publishing House, 1989), #894:

Our *Abba* in heaven,
hallowed be your name.

> Your kingdom come,
> Your will be done on earth as in heaven.
> Give us today our daily bread.
> Forgive us our sins
> as we forgive those who sin against us.
> Save us in the time of trial
> and deliver us from evil.
> For yours is the kingdom,
> and the power and the glory
> now and forever.
> Amen.

Luke records that one day as Jesus was finishing his time of prayer his disciples asked, "Lord, teach us to pray."

Jesus taught them what we call the Lord's Prayer or the Daily Prayer. It has the character of a daily prayer. The early church prayed it three times a day in the Jewish rhythm of morning, afternoon, and evening prayers (*Didache* 8:3). Here is a prayer for each and all of our days.

THE SHAPE

The shape of the Lord's Prayer has a beautiful simplicity and symmetry.[4] There is a beginning: "Our *Abba*, in heaven." There is an ending: "For yours is the kingdom and the power and the glory now and forever. Amen." And there are the two sets of three petitions. The first set of three is about God:

(1) Hallowed be your name

(2) Your kingdom come

(3) Your will be done
on earth as in heaven.

The second set of three is about us:

(1) Give us today our daily bread.

(2) Forgive us our sins
as we forgive those who sin against us.

(3) Save us in the time of trial
and deliver us from evil.

We begin the prayer with *God* rather than ourselves—a rather countercultural notion. The hallowing of God's name, the coming of God's kingdom, the doing of God's will. Then the prayer moves to our most basic human needs, which are of the greatest concern to God: our bread, our forgiveness and forgivingness, and our protection.

The simplicity of this prayer is part of its spiritual genius. The other part is how it encompasses all of what Jesus was about in the mission of the gospel. It is, as Tertullian described it in the second century, "a summary of the gospel." [5]

THE ADDRESS

Joachim Jeremias boldly wrote: "Jesus appeared in this world with a new prayer." [6] Jesus brought a new prayer and a new way of praying, and it begins with the word *Abba*. Various phrases of the prayer could have been prayed by any Jew of Jesus' day. It has many similarities with the *Kaddish*, as cited in the last chapter. What is new is how Jesus arranged the prayer and how it begins.

"*Abba*," Luke begins the prayer. Matthew begins, "Our *Abba*." The actual Greek word is *pater* or "father." Joachim Jeremias suggests that behind every "pater" on Jesus' lips in the Gospels in the

Greek New Testament is an echo of Jesus' Aramaic word *Abba*. Aramaic was Jesus' native tongue. Hebrew was the tongue of his religion and tradition. Growing up four miles from the bustling Greco-Roman city of Sepphoris, he may well have also known both Latin and Greek, but Aramaic was his everyday tongue. The Aramaic *Abba* was the word Jewish children and adults used for "father."

Joachim Jeremias influenced a generation of scholars with his conclusions:

> *We do not have a single example* of God being addressed as *Abba* in Judaism, but Jesus *always* addressed God in this way in his prayers.[7]

Current scholarship, qualifying his claims, is questioning the absolute uniqueness of Jesus' use of *Abba* as an address to God.[8] But there is little doubt that Jesus' use was startlingly novel. James D. G. Dunn writes: "When we 'listen in' on Jesus' prayers the distinctive word we hear is '*Abba.*'"[9]

Jeremias's early work suggested that a good translation of *Abba* might be "Daddy" or "Poppa" and that its derivation came from a child's earliest babbling words for father. While *Abba* could well have been babbled by children, current scholarship establishes that it first was an adult word for father in Aramaic or Hebrew.[10] The name conveyed both intimacy and respect. For Jesus it was an address that expressed a relationship of remarkable intimacy, trust, confidence, and affection.

The word "father" had other associations in the Hebrew tradition. God the liberator had freed his "firstborn son" from slavery in Egypt (Exodus 4:22-23). God the covenant maker had created a covenant relationship with Israel the son, Israel the daughter. But there appears something startlingly new about the way Jesus prayed to God as *Abba*. God is a parent who loves us perfectly, provides for us faithfully, and takes immense delight in us.

At Jesus' baptism the Spirit of God descended upon Jesus, and a voice from heaven said, "You are my Son, the Beloved; with you I am well pleased" (Mark 1:11 NRSV). This scene depicts the "*Abba-*

experience" which was, I believe, the heart of Jesus' spirituality. God delighted in Jesus; Jesus delighted in God.

But we do not stop there. Jesus said *we*, his disciples, could pray to God as *Abba* too: "Our *Abba* in heaven." This new way of praying was so central that the church felt that praying *Abba* was itself a manifestation of the Spirit of God and Spirit of Christ in them as they prayed (Galatians 4:6; Romans 8:15). *Abba, Abba, Abba*—there was an ecstatic character to its use, as the human soul merged with God's Spirit.

God is the child's *Abba*, the child freely, unself-consciously babbling God's name. God is Israel's *Abba*—a God saving and setting Israel free. God is the world's *Abba*, gracious provider of all there is, "the faithfulness at the heart of things." God is the disciples' *Abba*: In following Jesus, we discover our own belovedness.

Should we pray *Abba* as in Luke or "Our *Abba*" as in Matthew? Luke's *Abba* may be more original; often the shorter version of a passage is. But scholar James Barr cautions us from jumping to this conclusion.[11] "Our *Abba*" could just as easily been spoken by Jesus. Its sense is more consistent with the theology of the prayer. We pray *Abba* as part of a community and members together of God's whole creation. The kingdom of God is not just personal; it is social and communal. "Our *Abba*" better represents the character of the whole prayer.

"Our *Abba* in *heaven*." "Who art in heaven" reminds us that the God just pictured in the human analogy of a father and parent is beyond all we know of father, mother, parent.

Sometimes we use human analogies and earthly metaphors for God, saying: "God is like . . ." Other times we bow beneath the holy otherness of God and say, "God is not like . . ." Isaiah writes: "For my thoughts are not your thoughts, neither are your ways your ways, says the LORD" (Isaiah 55:8). "Who art in heaven" says that God is beyond even our best images for God.

Here is another reason I prefer to use *Abba* rather than "father." Its foreignness helps preserve the mystery of God and blurs, however slightly, the patriarchal sense of "pater." The strangeness of *Abba* slows us up as we read it and causes us to ask, *What did* Jesus *mean when he said* Abba?

"Father," or "Mother," as a name for God can be, depending on our experience, a window open to God or a shut door. *Abba* throws some mystery back into the word, as does the phrase "who art in heaven." God, who is like a father or mother, is also unlike any mother or father we know. *Our Abba in heaven.*

"Who art in heaven" preserves the holy otherness of God, but it should not signify God's remoteness: A God way up there, someone distant from us and from earth. Let us picture heaven as the realm of Spirit that interpenetrates the material realm of earth. Heaven is the Spirit realm unseen, intangible, yet, to use Reynolds Price's metaphor, "as real as music." The realm of heaven mingles with all created life and infuses creation itself.

Heaven is not the same as earth, as matter and spirit are not the same, but it enters matter as air enters our lungs and is carried on our blood to all parts of the body. Spirit upholds matter. It is life force; it is what Gandhi called "soul force." It is God breathing. If God stopped breathing the universe would stop.

"The kingdom is *within* you [*entos* you]," Jesus said, which means that heaven and its kingdom are that close, as close as your own breath.

"Our *Abba* in heaven," the prayer begins with Jesus' deepest sense of his belovedness and of our belovedness. God is *Abba* to us all. So we pray "Our *Abba* in heaven."

THE FIRST OF THE GOD-CENTERED PETITIONS: "HALLOWED BE YOUR NAME"

We do not pray to any god or to some generalized God: "To whom it may concern." We pray to a God specifically revealed to Israel and to Jesus. The name of God that Abraham used was "El Shaddai" or "God of the mountains," often translated "Almighty God" (an interesting and not altogether satisfying move from concrete image to abstract concept).

The name revealed to Moses as prelude to Exodus was the verb *YHWH*. We only guess at the word's pronunciation, "Yahweh." It is a form of the verb "to be." Its translation is elusive, but most translate it "I am who I am." Martin Buber translates it "I am there." [12] In traditional Judaism, God's name is not pronounced out of reverence. *Adonai* is substituted for God's name.

But *Adonai* is the title of a male authority figure ("Master"), and "Yahweh" has been thereby rendered "LORD" in subsequent translations of Scripture—from "I am," a verb, to "Lord," a male authority figure—think of the implications.

Liturgical theologian Gail Ramshaw after extensive study and reflection offers this translation of *Yahweh*: "Living One." [13] It is truer to the original dynamism of the name.

Why did God give Moses a name with an elusive meaning, wrapped in mystery, a name virtually untranslatable? I like the suggestion of Dr. Toni Craven, professor of Hebrew Bible at Brite Divinity School. When God gave this name to Moses, she says, God was saying, "My name is Yahweh. If you follow me I will teach you what this means." We learn God in the following of God.

When someone calls your name, you turn your head, almost without thinking. The Hebrew people drew back from saying God's name so they would not presume to control God by the use of God's name. It is easy to slip into a form of magical religion— where we think we can conjure God or control God by what we do or say. We are tempted to think or hope that by praying the right way long enough, often enough, God will turn, hear us, and answer us. Jesus taught, "You need not worry about trying to curry God's favor or get God's attention. God's ear is already inclined. God is already drawing near to help."

To hallow God's name is to turn from prayer as magic. *Yahweh* or *Abba* is not "abracadabra." To hallow God's name is to set it apart in our hearts and in our minds and on our lips, to set it apart and make it holy. It is to regard the name of God as the truest and dearest, highest and holiest of all names. There is one name before which we bow our heads, one name that causes us to kneel.

To hallow God's name is also to take up the cause of God, to dedicate oneself to what God is doing in the world so that God's name and character will be known throughout the world, and

God's healing work done. To have a friend is to take up their cause. God's great cause, the will of God for the world, was signified by Jesus by the phrase "kingdom of God." It was the main subject of his preaching.

> The time is ripe; the kingdom of God is at hand; turn and believe the good news. (Mark 1:15 AT)

It is there in the first petition of the Lord's Prayer: "Your kingdom come." It is to the kingdom and its coming to which we turn in the next chapter.

For now, relish the experience of being the beloved of God, whom you can call *Abba*. Brennan Manning tells the story of a Detroit priest who went on a two-week vacation to Ireland. His uncle there was about to celebrate his eightieth birthday. On that day the two got dressed and went on a hike along the shores of Lake Killarney. They stopped to watch the sunrise. Suddenly the uncle turned and went skipping down the road! He was radiant with joy. His nephew said, "Uncle Seamus, you look really happy."

"I am, lad."

"Want to tell me why?"

His uncle replied, "Yes, you see, me *Abba* is very fond of me."[14] And so is your *Abba* fond of you!

CHAPTER 3

The Lord's Prayer, Part 2

I n the last chapter we covered the address "Our *Abba* in heaven" and the first of the three God-centered petitions, "Hallowed be your name." Now we turn to the second and perhaps most pivotal of all the petitions, "Your kingdom come."

THE KINGDOM

The preaching of the kingdom was the heartbeat of Jesus' preaching:

> The time is ripe; the kingdom of God is at hand; turn and believe the good news. (Mark 1:15 AT)

The kingdom of God, or reign of God, is God's dream for this human, historical, material world: "on *earth* as in heaven." It is already true in God's eternity, but God wants a universe unified in the love of God and neighbor, which is its design and its destiny. Matthew's translation of Jesus' phrase "kingdom of God" into "kingdom of heaven," for reasons of reverence—not wanting to use God's name— has led us into a falsely "otherworldly" view of the kingdom.

The Hebrew prophets were captured by the dream of the kingdom, a vision of the world where God's justice and peace would reign:

- Where swords would be beaten into plowshares and spears into pruning hooks and we would learn war no more

- Where there would be equity for the poor, help for the weak, and liberty to the captives

- Where justice would roll down like waters and righteousness like an overflowing stream

- Where everyone would sit safely under his or her fig tree, and no one would be afraid

- Where the earth would be full of the knowledge of the Lord as the waters cover the sea

We must take care not to forget the *earthliness* of God's kingdom—and its claim upon us to create a world more fair and hospitable, where justice is embodied personally and systematically, and where peace is hammered out in hope.

Jesus came preaching the nearness of the kingdom with its glad and urgent invitation to us all. "The kingdom of God is *in* you, *among* you [*entos* you in the Greek] in your midst" (Luke 17:21 AT). The kingdom is here not there, near not far, as close as your own breath, closer.

But the kingdom requires a turning, a *metanoia*, a repentance. "You must change your life" is its insistent call. There has to be an entering in, a letting go, for the kingdom is near but not fully come.

Think of the kingdom as a circle that overlaps the circle of our earthly existence, but only partially. The petition "Your kingdom come" prays for the reign of God to overtake our existence, make it new, make it right, and make it whole.

It is a dangerous prayer: "Your kingdom come, your will be done on earth, in *me*, as in heaven." It lets God loose in us and in the life of the world.

The Celtic Christian symbol for the Holy Spirit is the wild goose. What a startlingly different image than that of the heavenly dove! We pray for the wild goose of a Spirit to lead us out where we need to go—and where God needs for us to go. We will not return unchanged. The poet Mary Oliver writes, "Tell me what you plan to do with / your one wild and precious life?"[1] So God asks us, and so we pray this prayer with all its hidden wildness: "Your kingdom come!"

GOD'S WILL

Your will be done
on earth as in heaven.

Here is the third of the God-centered petitions. It is troublesome because our humankind easily presumes to know what the will of God is. "Deus lo vult"—God wills it—was the rallying cry of Pope Urban in 1095 as he began the Crusades, a two-hundred-year war against the Muslims. "Allah wills it" is the mantra of the twenty-first-century Muslim terrorist as he flies a suicide mission into skyscrapers.

We should note that at this point the one who prays is praying only for *God* to do God's will. We are not presuming that we perfectly know God's will, or that we can bring in the kingdom by human hands alone.

The New Testament claims that we have been given a glimpse of the mystery of God's will in Jesus Christ. He is the "open secret" of God's will, says the apostle Paul. And what is the purpose, the will, the good pleasure of God?: "To unite all things in him, things in heaven and things on earth" (Ephesians 1:10).

American poet, novelist, and essayist Wendell Berry offers a remarkable rephrasing of the idea of the kingdom of God. He calls it "The Great Economy," where all things spiritual and material, human and creaturely are woven together and brought into right relation with one another. The first principle of the kingdom of God is "that it includes everything."[2] It orders and encompasses all our smaller economies. To pray "Your will be done" is to pray that "The Great Economy" be restored by human and divine hands joined.

DAILY BREAD

This first of the three "us" petitions is, "Give us this day our daily bread." Here is not a selfish prayer, but one of the greatest simplicity. It does not say, "Give us this day our filet mignon with béarnaise sauce." Or, "Give me today bread enough to last me the rest of my life." Rather, "Give me bread sufficient for this day."

There is an echo here of the manna miracle in the wilderness when God provided the Hebrew people a curious white substance for food on their journey from slavery in Egypt to the promised land. "Manna" literally means "What's that?"—an apt name for that strange substance. They discovered that manna spoiled after one day. It could not be stored, only eaten the day of its provision. With that same dependence on God we pray, "Give us this day bread for today."

Our prayers can become anxious and greedy—the spiritual etiology of greed is often anxiety. But Jesus taught and lived a more trusting, less grasping way:

> Do not be anxious about your life, what you shall eat . . . nor about your body, what you shall put on. . . . Look at the birds of the air. . . . Consider the lilies of the field [God provides for them and will provide for you]. Therefore do not be anxious about tomorrow. (Matthew 6:25, 26, 28, 34)

There is a connection between the simplicity of this prayer and the call of God's kingdom for justice and compassion. As Gandhi is quoted: "There is enough in this world for everyone's need, but not enough for everyone's greed." Our anxiety-fed greed can close our hearts to our neighbor. I like very much the Argentine blessing set to music:

> God bless to us our bread
> And give bread to all those who are hungry
> And hunger for justice to those who are fed.
> God bless to us our bread.[3]

FORGIVENESS

The second of the "us" petitions is: "Forgive us our sins as we forgive those who sin against us." We could well use Matthew's word, "debts." It is closest to the word Jesus probably used, the Aramaic *hoba*. Sin always creates indebtedness. And the economic sin of injustice creates a social world of debt that is far from the way God intended. We could use the word Matthew used in Matthew 6:14, "trespasses," for sin implies a crossing of boundaries, an invasion of another's sacred personhood, a transgressing of God's plan for creation. We use here Luke's more general word, "sin" (Luke 11:4). While the word "sin" may evoke a scalding and toxic sense of shame, it has the virtue of communicating clearly and broadly. It also keeps in our spiritual vocabulary a word our world wants too easily to dismiss. The jolt it carries is purposive.

As much as daily bread, we need daily forgiveness. So Jesus follows the petition for daily bread with one for forgiveness. We can die from a lack of forgiveness—the kind we need to give and the kind we need to receive—as surely as from a lack of bread. This prayer can save our lives. A paraphrase of the Lord's Prayer set to the African American folk tune "Kum Ba Ya" connects bread and forgiveness and the dailyness of our need for both:

> Give us daily bread, day by day,
> And forgive our sins, day by day,
> As we too forgive day by day.
> O Lord, hear our prayer.

There was a startling gratuity, a radical giftedness to the for-giveness that Jesus taught and gave. It went out to all people, many of whom Jesus' religion and culture had placed beyond the reach of God's mercy. And it came not requiring repentance as a precondition, but *bringing* it in its healing wings.

Jesus pictured the forgiveness of God as the prodigal love of a father running to welcome home a wayward son. And before the boy can get his carefully rehearsed speech of repentance out of his mouth, his father is kissing and kissing him, wrapping his arms around him and calling for a homecoming feast. God's forgiveness is already on the way to us. Our prayer flings open the door to God's healing mercy: "Forgive us our sins."

What about the next phrase: "As we forgive those who sin against us"? Is there a conditionality about this prayer? It is not a legalistic conditionality: God waiting to see if we forgive before forgiving us. If so, who would be forgiven?

There is, however, a spiritual circle of conditionality: God's forgiveness loosens our hearts to forgive others; but if we refuse to forgive others, we stop the flow of God's forgiveness to us.

Picture the heart with a double-hinged door that swings in and swings out. As the door swings in, God's forgiveness flows in. But if we shut the door so that forgiveness does not flow back out to others, the door is frozen not only to the forgiveness we might give but also to the flow of God's forgiveness to us.

Forgiveness is learning to live in the free mercy of God. It is a letting go of our compulsion to control. Our refusal to forgive another who has hurt us may be the last bit of control we think we have over him or her. But this kind of thinking binds us as much as the other, maybe more.

Forgiveness is also letting go of the past that binds us. It is the step when once and for all you give up your attempts to make the past different. The past cannot be changed; it can only be forgiven. Forgiveness can help us "re-remember" the past, to put it back together, which is what the word "remember" means, to glimpse it in a new and kinder light. It helps us look with deeper understand-ing, under a new mercy, at the harm we've done or the one who has harmed us. It opens to us a future not dictated to us by the past.

Forgiveness may be the most difficult and most complex of life's spiritual challenges. C. S. Lewis wrote:

> Last week, while at prayer, I suddenly discovered—or felt as if I did—that I had really forgiven someone I have been trying to forgive for over thirty years. Trying, and praying that I might. [4]

"Forgive us our sins, as we forgive those who sin against us." As we pray this prayer day by day, we learn to swing the door more fully and freely in and out, letting more of God's forgiveness in and letting more forgiveness flow out to others.

PROTECTION FROM TEMPTATION AND EVIL

The last of the "us" petitions is for protection from the snares of temptation and from the assault of evil. All translations are interpretations. The translation I prefer is:

> Save us in the time of trial
> and deliver us from evil.

Ever since the prayer began to be prayed by followers of Jesus, people have stumbled over the phrase "Lead us not into temptation." Does the phrase suggest that sometimes God *does* lead us into temptation? The phrase was confusing enough that before the New Testament was even finished the book of James felt it important to say, perhaps with this issue in mind, "Let no one say when . . . tempted: 'I am tempted by God'; for God . . . tempts no one" (James 1:13). Later Latin manuscripts tried to help out by translating the petition: "Do not permit us to be led into temptation." I prefer the translation, "Save us in the time of trial" (*United Methodist Hymnal*, #894).

Fourteenth-century British anchorite Julian of Norwich heard

Jesus saying to her in this petition, "Thou shalt not be overcome." [5] Such is the heart of the petition: When tests come, keep me strong.

Most scholars agree that the word we have translated "temptation"—*peirasmon*—is better translated "test" or "trial." In times of testing or trial we are called upon to prove our true identity and character, who we are and whose we are. Sometimes the temptation comes in the form of sin; other times it comes as a time of great difficulty or suffering; other times it is a life-changing moment of choice, choice between two paths, good and evil, or between the good and the best. Will we in this moment of trial be true to God? Will we be true to our best self?

A Jewish evening prayer of Jesus' day may help us understand better this petition:

> Bring me not into sin, or into iniquity,
> or into temptation. And may our
> good inclination (yetzer ha*tov*)
> hold sway over me, and let not the
> evil inclination (yetzer ha*ra*) have
> sway over me.

As in the Lord's Prayer we have this Hebrew idiom: "Lead me not" or "bring me not" into temptation. It really means "do not let me be overcome" by temptation or sin. So we pray, "Save us in the time of trial."

The evening prayer also emphasizes that in any time of trial or testing we have a choice between the good impulse and the bad impulse. We are essentially good, but we can be pulled in either direction. We pray to stay true to God's way, for the best self to prevail over the false self. To use the language of Abraham Lincoln in his First Inaugural Address, we pray for "the better angels of our nature" to prevail.

If we are human we will face temptation, trial, tests. It goes with the territory. So we pray: When temptation comes, make us strong.

TEMPTATIONS

Let's look back at the temptations Jesus faced in the wilderness. They were a test of who he was and what he was called to be and do in this world.

The first temptation by the devil was for Jesus to turn stones into bread. Here is the temptation to make the material world the final realm. Physical hunger is important to God, but for us there is a deeper hunger. So Jesus answered by quoting Hebrew Scripture: "One does not live by bread alone, but by every word that comes from the mouth of God" (Matthew 4:4 NRSV).

The material is not the ultimate realm. Andy Warhol, pop culture icon, epitomized our age of materialism when he remarked that if he were to come back in another life he'd like to return as a ring on Elizabeth Taylor's finger. The terrorist attack on the World Trade Towers, September 11, 2001, was an attack on the economic structure of our nation and the community of nations. But as important as economic structures are to the well-being of the world and therefore to God, who cares about our physical well-being, there is another even more crucial realm, the realm of the Spirit. We do not live by bread alone.

The second temptation was to power. The devil showed Jesus all the nations of the world and said, "They are yours if you but fall down and worship me." Jesus again quoted scripture, "You shall worship the Lord your God and [God] only shall you serve" (Matthew 4:10).

The second temptation asks, *What will you trade for power and its prerequisites of fame and fortune? If you do have power, fame, fortune, influence, how will you use these? In service of good or evil?*

The third temptation was more subtle. The devil led Jesus to the pinnacle of the temple. He invited him to jump off and quoted Psalm 91:11-12 to him: "Don't you know God's angels will parachute you safely to the ground?" Evil quotes Scripture too.

Jesus said, relying again on God's Word, "Do not put the Lord your God to the test" (Matthew 4:7 NRSV).

The final temptation was to magical thinking. We say, "I am

unique, singular, special; the normal laws and rules of life do not apply to me." We believe reality applies to others, not to us. But if we jump off a bridge, gravity works 100 percent of the time. If we drink a quart of whiskey in an hour, we will poison our body. Moreover, we are not immune to suffering or to death. To run from suffering and death may be to run from life and from the highest of what we are called to do and to be.

Luke's temptation scene ends with these words:

> And when the devil had ended every temptation, he departed from him until an opportune time. (Luke 4:13)

The devil is an equal-opportunity seducer, an evil and opportunistic disease that waits until the right moment of vulnerability to attack. So we should pray every day, "Save us in the time of trial."

The tests, trials, temptations will come, some by way of the evil one, some by way of our own stumbling—but God is with us there too, even in our stumbling—some as part and parcel of the human condition. These are soul-making moments, times of spiritual formation and reformation. We therefore pray, "Save us in the time of trial."

EVIL

The last petition of the prayer ends, "And deliver us from evil." Or as some manuscripts have it, "from the evil one." Here is a jolt of realism from Jesus at the end of the prayer. Jesus recognized a malevolent power at work in the world, and he knew that apart from the power of God we could be overwhelmed by this evil.

Sometimes the evil is within us; other times it comes from without. We pray to be *delivered from the evil we would do and from what evil can do to us.*

There is a mystery to the presence of evil in the world, a mystery we cannot explain but which enters into our world through the freedom that God has placed in the fabric of the universe, a freedom that allows the wonderful and the terrible to happen.

Evil is that which destroys life and demeans persons. It creates lies and thrives on falsehood and deceit. In his book *People of the Lie*, Scott Peck says that human evil happens when we project our inner shadow, inner darkness onto others. Such is the importance of what AA calls a "fearless moral inventory." Part of C. S. Lewis's road to conversion came as the Spirit gave him an honest picture of his own inner darkness.

> For the first time I examined myself with a seriously practical purpose. And there I found what appalled me; a zoo of lusts, a bedlam of ambitions, a nursery of fears, a harem of fondled hatreds. My name was legion. [6]

Unless we are honest about ourselves we can project our inner darkness onto others and do them violence.

Evil can take hold of institutions and groups of people and cause individuals to do what they would never do as individuals, apart from the group. The New Testament calls these suprapersonal powers that can be overtaken by evil "principalities and powers."

Jesus was not naïve about the power and presence of evil. He saw the kingdom of God laying siege to the strongholds of evil, whether that evil was in the human heart and mind, or whether it was imbedded in social systems of oppression and exploitation. No wonder the New Testament says that it was these powers that be, the "rulers of this age" who put Jesus to death (1 Corinthians 2:8).

But Jesus' way of attacking the powers of evil was through a nonviolent resistance to evil. Resistance is necessary, else evil progress, but the mode of resistance is nonviolent. Jesus forswore violence as a way of defeating violence. He chose not to join the justice and freedom movements of his day that used violent means to achieve their ends.

"Love your enemy," he said. "Do not return evil for evil." The words must have been as hard to hear in his day as in ours. How are we to follow such a one as he when we suffer evil done to us, when we see the powers of evil do their worst in our world today? There are no glib answers. To be sure, we cannot answer for others whose plight may be much worse than ours. But we are called to answer with and for our own lives.

The answer comes as we pray Jesus' prayers after Jesus, with Jesus. Do you remember the prayers Jesus prayed while being executed on a Roman cross? We will discuss them later, but hear them now, three of them, a prayer of forgiveness, a cry of desolation, a prayer of relinquishment: The prayer of forgiveness: "*Abba,* forgive them; for they know not what they do." The honest, agonized cry of abandonment: "Eli, Eli, lama sabach-tha-ni?" that is, "My God, my God, why hast thou forsaken me?" The prayer of relinquishment: "*Abba,* into your hands I commit my spirit!"

These are prayers that trust our lives into the hands of God. When darkness is so thick we cannot see the way, when evil seems stronger than life itself, we find by faith our way into the prayer:

> Save us in the time of trial
> and deliver us from evil.

Then at that moment when it seems darkest, the prayer issues into the impossible possibility of praise. Doxology breaks as the dawn.

> For yours is the kingdom
> and the power and the glory
> now and forever. Amen.

For over five years of Thursdays, my Fort Worth congregation and I invited the homeless of the city to a family-style meal where we ate together around tables with cut flowers, table cloths, real plates, and identifiable meats. After we gained their trust they came in droves, around two hundred every week. Over those years we ate together, worshiped together, and became friends.

Often our homeless friends would bring their friends from the streets. It was for some the only good meal of the week and the only one eaten in the safety of friends. It was for many their weekly "church."

Part of the premeal words that were said to one another included the Lord's Prayer. One evening one of our regulars brought a few friends. As we came near the part where we said the Lord's Prayer together, he punched his friends on either side and said in a loud whisper all at the table could hear: "Here it comes!" This prayer was as much his food as what he was about to be served. He needed to say these words and needed to pray them alongside others who needed and wanted to pray them too.

So do we. That prayer, prayed often, prayed with others, can save a person's life.

CHAPTER 4

Prayer amid Life's Reversals

P raising, that's it! He was as one appointed to praise."[1] Or, in another translation, "Praise was his mission." So wrote the poet Rilke in his *Sonnets to Orpheus*. And so I think about Jesus. We see it in this prayer in Matthew 11:

> I thank you, *Abba*,
> Lord of heaven and earth,
> that you have hidden these things
> from the wise and learned
> and revealed them to little ones;
> yes, *Abba*, such was your gracious will. (NRSV, adapted)

Praise and thanksgiving pervaded Jesus' life. The poet Denise Levertov writes that without a passionate love of life and the poetry of praise we do not have the energy to help our world. "Sing awe," she urges. "Breathe out praise."[2] William Morris once wrote about people who cultivate "unhappiness as a fine art." In contrast, Jesus sang awe, breathed out praise.

There is a sculpture in Santa Fe that leaves me stunned with gladness every time I see it. The first time I saw it I thought I was looking at a wild, angular Saint Francis. Its long, long arms are extended, and birds are flying all around him. It is in fact a sculpture of Elijah being fed by the birds in the wilderness. But it also calls to mind Francis of Assisi rapt in his ecstatic praise, even as he faced death:

> All creatures of our God and King,
> Lift up your voice and with us sing,
> Alleluia, Alleluia.

And it calls to mind Jesus praising the God of the birds and wild-flowers and the Galilean sea, the *Abba* of all life.

There was a "wild gratitude" about Jesus, wild in its exultation, wild in its constancy through all life's seasons, like the wild gratitude captured by Edward Hirsch in his poem about the British poet Christopher Smart locked away in an insane asylum but who wrote joyously beautiful poetry to God. Smart, wrote Hirsch:

> . . . wanted to kneel down and pray without ceasing
> In every one of the splintered London streets,
>
> And was locked away in the madhouse at St. Luke's
> With his sad religious mania, and his wild gratitude,
> And his grave prayers for the other lunatics,
> And his great love for his speckled cat, Jeoffry.[3]

Jesus must have had such as Christopher Smart in mind when he prayed to *Abba*, and when he gave these beatitudes:

> You that are destitute rejoice: our father's
>   kingdom shall be yours.
> Rejoice, you that are hungry: you shall feast.
> You that weep: you shall laugh with joy.
> Rejoice, you that are persecuted: our father
>   knows you and you will know him.[4]

Such was the gratitude of Jesus, born in his trust in *Abba*.

One sees Jesus' gratitude in the fourfold action that was his blessing at mealtime: He took bread, blessed it, broke it, and gave it to his disciples. The same fourfold action happened as he ate with friends, as he fed the multitude, at his last Passover meal with disciples, and in his resurrection appearances with disciples.

On Easter Sunday evening, Jesus appeared incognito to the two disciples along a road to Emmaus. They did not recognize him by his appearance, or even as he explained Scripture to them. But that night as they sat at table, he took the bread and blessed it and broke it and gave it to them; and their eyes were opened and they knew who he was. Known by his gratitude.

"I thank you, *Abba*" was the systole and diastole of his heart. He gave thanks for the sun and the rain graciously given by God to all. He gave thanks for good food and the company of friends, for flying birds and the songs God stamped in their throats, for the wildflowers strewn across Galilean hillsides. "I thank you, God, Lord of the universe," he prayed as a good Jew, for the wheat that springs green from the earth and makes this bread, for the grapes full and sweet in the vine that provide wine to gladden our hearts.

We have been given too ascetic a picture of Jesus; he was not life-denying but life-affirming. Once he was chastised because he did not teach his disciples to fast as did John the Baptist and the Pharisees. Jesus said, "Can you make wedding guests fast while the bridegroom is with them?" (Luke 5:34). Which means, " Yes, there is a time to fast, in time of sorrow and mourning, but now is a time to feast." He was called "a glutton and drunkard, friend of tax-collectors and sinners." A holy man should not enjoy the company of sinners—a holy man should not enjoy anything! This man is too happy; he has too much joy! When the wedding feast at Cana ran out of wine and the host was miserable with embarrassment, Jesus turned water into wine, 180 gallons or so (John 2:1-12). We have no stingy God. Jesus joyed in such a God.

Jesus had his mission to save, but praise, too, was his mission. E. B. White once wrote:

> If the world were merely seductive, that would be
> easy. If it were merely challenging that would be no
> problem. But I arise every morning, torn between a
> desire to save the world and to savour the world. That
> makes it hard to plan the day.[5]

Jesus came not just to save the world but also to savor it. If you do not love the world, and savor it, why would it be worth saving?

What is extraordinary about the prayer from Matthew 11—and I think it is as clear a glimpse as we have of Jesus in the Gospels—is that it is a prayer of thanksgiving prayed in face of a baffling and crushing reversal of expectations.

> I thank you, *Abba*,
> Lord of heaven and earth,
> that you have hidden these things
> from the wise and learned
> and revealed them to little ones;
> yes, *Abba*, such was your gracious will [your *eudokia*, your good pleasure]. (NRSV, adapted)

Jesus had come to renew and reform his beloved Jewish faith, not to replace it,

> Think not that I have come to abolish the law and the prophets; I have come not to abolish but to fulfill them. (Matthew 5:17)

Even at age twelve he was in the temple of Jerusalem astounding the teachers of Israel with "his understanding and his answers" (Luke 2:47).

Jesus might well have expected and hoped for the teachers and leaders of his nation to hear and join him in his renewal movement. But that did not happen. This prayer was prayed when what was happening was becoming obvious and humanly irreversible. The wise and learned were saying no, and the little ones of his day were saying yes.

Jesus preached the drawing near of God's kingdom, but such preaching was a threat to the religious, social, and political status quo, as it is today. Saint Augustine once prayed: "O God, make me chaste, but not yet!"—a prayer with which we might identify. We are inclined to pray: "O God, bring your kingdom—your kingdom come—but not yet!"

We should not read into Jesus' prophetic program of renewal an anti-Jewish tone. What we have is the prophetic bias against established religion that hoards the blessings of God and turns the grace of God into sacraments to be carefully dispensed.

Jesus preached what John Dominic Crossan has termed in his arresting phrase "a brokerless kingdom."[6] The blessings of God are given freely to all people, good and bad, religious and nonreligious, a grace unbrokered by priest, temple, mosque, or church that sometimes act as if they have God's exclusive franchise of grace.

The religious leaders were threatened by Jesus' teaching of an unbrokered kingdom. The political leaders saw his teaching and popular following as destabilizing to the order of things. So the wise and learned, blinded by their position, their privilege, their power, were saying no to Jesus. A Harvard degree, a seminary doctorate, a Stanford Ph.D. do not guarantee a good soul; nor do they automatically produce wisdom, compassion, and good sense.

There was a no, but simultaneously, there was this joyous yes coming from those Jesus called the *nepioi*, the infants, babes, little ones. The Greek word sometimes refers to infants, other times to "little ones" in a broader sense: the weak, the poor, the simple, the unlearned, the needy.[7]

In the surprising ways of God, God was using *nepioi* to carry the gospel! "Unless you turn and become as children," Jesus said, that is, those weak enough, small enough, needy enough to receive the kingdom as a gift, "you will never enter the kingdom of heaven" (Matthew 18:3).

Jesus saw the unexpected turn: The no of the wise and powerful, the yes of the poor and weak. He had to know what this meant—his rejection and probable death. But he prays:

> I thank you, *Abba,*
> Lord of heaven and earth,
> that you have hidden these things
> from the wise and learned
> and revealed them to little ones;
> yes, *Abba,* such was your *eudokia.* (NRSV, adapted)

Eudokia is a beautiful word that means "good pleasure," or "gracious will." *Eudokia* does not mean that everything that happens is willed and orchestrated by God. It means that God somehow uses everything for God's good purpose, the healing of our lives and the healing of the nations. Jesus says unequivocally in Matthew, "It is not the will of my Father who is in heaven that one of these little ones should perish" (Matthew 18:14). And he said to his anxious disciples, "Fear not, little flock, for it is your *Abba's* good pleasure to give you the kingdom" (Luke 12:32 RSV, adapted).

Paul describes the *eudokia* of God revealed in Jesus Christ to be this, "To unite all things ... things in heaven, things on earth" (Ephesians 1:9-10). This is the will of God, the purpose of God, the good pleasure of God—and when we are in synch with this purpose of God, we feel God's pleasure, even when we go through very difficult times.

Jesus' trust in the *eudokia* of God let him give thanks amid the ruins. It also led him to offer a new way that involved the love of enemy.

When Jesus commanded us to love our enemies, there was a theological basis for this command that we often miss:

> Love your enemies and pray for those who persecute you, so that you may be sons and daughters of your *Abba* who is in heaven; *for God makes the sun to rise on the evil and on the good, and sends rain on the just and on the unjust.* (Matthew 5:44-45 AT)

We are commanded to love our enemies because *God* does so— and God shows it by pouring out the blessings of life upon all. Reinhold Niebuhr described this character of God as the "impartial goodness [of God] beyond good and evil."[8] As Niebuhr noted, the philosopher Berdyaev called forgiveness "the morality beyond morality," for it at the same time fulfills and transcends our human concepts of justice. So the providence of God, shown in the sun and the rain itself, demonstrates a morality beyond morality. The impartial goodness of God pours out blessings on all people with no special favors. And I would add with no special immunity from harm for those who are good. I wish I could see it otherwise. If you remember from the temptation of Jesus, it was the *devil* who offered Jesus special immunity from harm.

But I cannot stop there. As people of faith, we trust, however difficult at times, in the moral basis of the universe where justice, love, and peace will prevail over violence, cruelty, and injustice.

Martin Luther King, Jr., used to reassure his African American community in its fight for justice by saying that the arc of the moral universe bends slowly toward justice—but it *does bend* toward justice. God's justice is at work, though not necessarily by our means nor according to our timetable.

What we say about our lives—emotionally, economically, politically, spiritually—is this: *Things are beyond our control but are not out of control.* There is One guiding us and our world through the turns and travail of our days toward the *eudokia* of God, the uniting of all things in heaven and on earth. Our lives may not go as we plan, or as we hope, but we pray with Jesus as he himself faced reversal of expectation:

> I thank you, *Abba,*
> Lord of heaven and earth,
> that you have hidden these things
> from the wise and learned
> and revealed them to the little ones;
> yes, *Abba,* such was your gracious will. (NRSV, adapted)

We may walk through difficult times for awhile, but we will walk together. Jesus' prayer reminds me of the prayer I heard quoted by Max Cleland, then head of the Veterans Administration under President Carter. Cleland is a Vietnam veteran, a triple amputee, and an extraordinary man. The prayer he quoted was attributed to an injured Civil War soldier:

> I asked God for strength that I might achieve;
> I was made weak that I might learn humbly to obey.
> I asked for help that I might do greater things;
> I was given infirmity that I might do better things.

I asked for riches that I might be happy;
I was given poverty that I might be wise.
I asked for power that I might have the praise of
    men;
I was given weakness that I might feel the need of
    God.
I asked for all things that I might enjoy life;
I was given life that I might enjoy all things.
I got nothing I asked for, but everything I hoped for.
Almost despite myself my unspoken prayers were
    answered.
I among all men am most richly blessed.

"I thank you, *Abba*," Jesus prayed as the tide turned against him, for he had glimpsed the ocean.

CHAPTER 5

The Gethsemane Prayer: Thy Will Be Done

Abba, *all things are possible to you;*
remove this cup from me;
yet not what I want, but what you want.—Mark 14:36
NRSV, adapted

Mark's Gospel, the earliest one written, is the only one to capture Jesus' use of *Abba* in his Aramaic tongue. It is here in the Gethsemane prayer: "*Abba*, all things are possible to you."

Earlier in the Daily Prayer, Jesus had taught his disciples to pray: "Your kingdom come, your will be done." Now in the garden of Gethsemane, the night of his arrest, the eve of his death, came its moment of truth. "Do I mean this prayer?"

At this moment Jesus knew his arrest and death were imminent. Jesus' preaching of the kingdom had gotten caught in a vortex of political, social, and religious paranoia, and people saw his death as a way out of danger. The mechanism of sacred violence by which a people believe the sacrifice of someone's life will save the whole was in full swing.

Jesus' prayer was the agonized cry of one who knew this was the last moment to turn from death's path. Can one imagine a fiercer inner conflict than this, to preserve one's life or to offer it up in the inscrutable hope that God will somehow use it for the good of the world? So in agony he prayed to God, his *Abba:*

> *Abba,* all things are possible to you;
> remove this cup from me;
> yet not what I want, but what you want.

Luke's version has the more familiar cadences: "Not my will, but thine, be done" (Luke 22:42). There is the intimate address, *Abba.* There is the expression of trust in the power and goodness of God, "All things are possible to you." There is the acknowledgment of the clash between the will to live and the will to serve God's highest purpose; and there is the offering of one's life into God's purposes, "Yet not what I want, but what you want."

As we flesh out the entire scene the drama is only intensified. Jesus took his disciples to the garden. He asked them to sit while he prayed. Here was another instance of Jesus needing sustained, solitary prayer. He then asked Peter, James, and John to go with him to the place of prayer. These three were chosen by Jesus to be with him at other key moments, such as at the Transfiguration (Mark 9:2-13).

The text says next that Jesus was "greatly distressed and troubled" (Mark 14:33). Raymond Brown comments that the Greek verb for "distressed" connotes profound physical and emotional disarray, "a shuddering horror," and that the Greek verb "troubled" conveys deepest anguish.[1] The other Gospels soften or omit this picture of Jesus as one at such desperate a place.

Jesus then said to his disciples, "My soul is very sorrowful, even unto death; remain here and watch" (Mark 14:34). The call to stay awake and be watchful had more to do than with simply not falling asleep. More is needed than extra caffeine.

Then the text says he went a bit farther, "he fell on the ground and prayed that, if it were possible, the hour might pass from him" (v. 35). Then the prayer, *"Abba . . ."* Matthew's Gospel says that three times Jesus prayed this prayer. Three times signifies a long agonized night of prayer. Luke's Gospel says that "his sweat became like great drops of blood falling down on the ground" (Luke 22:44 NRSV).

Jesus prayed to the God he trusted utterly. He prayed honestly to be spared an excruciating and humiliating execution on a Roman cross. He prayed for God to intervene and make some new way in this crisis so he wouldn't have to die this way. He could have chosen to run from this scene and escape death this way, but the integrity of his life and mission would not permit him to do so.

So with one breath he begged his God to find another way, and with the next breath he submitted himself to the train of events, whatever they proved to be. He would be true to his calling—and to the way of the kingdom he preached. God had used his life for the kingdom's sake; if death were to come, God could use his death too.

Remove this cup . . . yet not what I want, but what you want.

This prayer forces us to the ground floor of our belief. It portrays the utter freedom of the person and the utter freedom of God. Jesus knows he is free to go ahead with a martyr and savior's death or to flee that death. He believes that God may yet find a way to fulfill the kingdom's purpose other than by his death. The Hebrew Scriptures are replete with people of faith praying to God, hoping God will change God's mind—and God doing exactly that.

In the radical openness of God's universe and of God's continuing creation and redemption of it, prayer is a way of discerning our human participation with God in creation and redemption. It is sometimes an honest cry to ask God to find another way. It is an act of deep trustfulness to follow our best discernment of God's will even if that means suffering and death.

On one level it is morally absurd to think God would "will" or "want" Jesus' death. This would make God a monster. Remember, it was Jesus who said, "It is not the will of my *Abba* that one of these little ones should perish" (Matthew 18:14). The phrase "God's will" has been used to cover the most horrendous and heartbreaking of events, from the tragic death of the young to natural catastrophe to the sacred violence of crusades. Again, God's true will is the uniting and healing of all things (Ephesians 1:9-10; Revelation 21:1-2). It is *shalom*, well-being and peace.

Moreover, in the kingdom of God that Jesus preached and embodied, the means must be consistent with ends. The ends are present in the means, so Jesus chose nonviolence as the way. You just can't kill for Jesus or in the name of God, whether that name is Yahweh, Allah, or *Abba*.

The powers of evil call for resistance from God's people, but we are always tempted to become evil in order to defeat evil. As the saying goes, "Be careful whom you call enemy. You may become them." Jesus was willing at this point to *give* his life; he was not willing to take life.

In John's Gospel Jesus is interrogated by Pontius Pilate the Roman procurator. He inquires about Jesus' being called "king of the Jews." He wonders what Jesus' *modus operandi* might be. Jesus responds:

> My kingship is not of this world; if my kingship were of this world, my servants would fight. . . . But my kingship is not from the world. (John 18:36)

These words of Jesus do not imply an overly spiritualized kingdom disconnected from the real world. They describe a kingdom with the goals of transforming the world without the violent and coercive means the world has adopted.

We should hear this prayer in the broader context of the Lord's Prayer: "Thy kingdom come, thy will be done on earth as in heaven." Jesus offers his will, his life, to the ultimate purposes of God.

When Jesus knelt in the garden he knew that his preaching and living of the kingdom had brought him to a final clash with the powers that be and their resistance to God's kingdom. Who wants to die, especially this one who loved life as much as anyone who ever lived? But now to refuse death would be to deny all he had lived for. James Hillman considers the death of Socrates, who himself felt bound to his death: "His death belonged to the integrity of his image, to his innate form."[2] And so did Jesus' death belong to the integrity of his personhood and the integrity of the way God had chosen to redeem the world—not through the power of the sword but through the power of love made eloquent in suffering.

Following his prayer, Jesus returned to the three, Peter, James, and John, and found them asleep. Jesus said to Peter, "Simon, are you asleep? Could you not keep awake one hour? Keep awake and pray that you may not come into the time of trial" (Mark 14:37-38 NRSV). These words are a call to prayer that leads us back to the petition of the Lord's Prayer, "Save us in the time of trial and deliver us from evil." The key words that unite these words with other teachings of Jesus are, "Watch and pray that you may not enter into temptation" (Mark 14:38).

Watchfulness is a form of prayer. Prayer keeps us watchful. What we wish to be alert to is the lure of temptation, the time of testing and trial. The Greek word for temptation is again, as in the Lord's Prayer, *peirasmon.* Keep awake and pray lest you enter into temptation, trial, testing.

C. P. Snow's provocatively titled book *The Sleep of Reason* is taken from the title of one of Goya's etchings, *El sueño de la razon produce monstruos*: "The sleep of reason brings forth monsters." Jesus rouses us from spiritual sleep to spiritual watchfulness. Prayer is what alerts us to the presence of evil in all its forms, monstrous and banal. It keeps us from giving up our sacred personhood and becoming capable of monstrous acts.

In south-central Kentucky is the Abbey of Gethsemani where Thomas Merton lived. The brothers have built a "garden of Gethsemane" out in the woods. When you approach it, you see first a memorial plaque. The garden is erected in memory of Jonathan Daniels, a young seminarian who was murdered in the Civil Rights movement of the 1960s. This is no sentimental journey. Then you come to a sculpture, life-size, of the three disciples. They are reclined against one another, dead asleep.

Then you go around a bend in the woods and see the solitary

agonized figure of Christ kneeling on a hard stone. (How long could one kneel like that?) His head is not bowed in pious resignation; his hands are not folded in proper prayer. His head is thrown back in agony, his hands cover his face. With his head thrown back you see his neck, a strong, sinewy neck, exposed to earth and heaven.

This is how Jesus came to the garden, offered his prayer to his *Abba*, prayed for some other way, then yielded himself in deep willingness to the purposes of God, which he could barely see but trusted with his life.

He asks us to watch and pray so that in our hardest hours of testing and trial we will be true to God and to our best, truest self.

CHAPTER 6

Prayers from the Cross

T he sayings of Jesus spoken from the cross have been col-
lected as "the seven last words of Christ."[1] Three of them
were prayers. Flannery O'Connor wrote:

> The man in the violent situation reveals those quali-
> ties least dispensable in his personality, those quali-
> ties which are all he will have to take into eternity
> with him.[2]

What did Jesus pray in the violent situation of the cross? He prayed
a prayer for forgiveness, a cry of desolation, and a prayer of relinquishment. As we face the worst life can offer—terrorists flying aircraft into the World Trade Towers, betrayal at the hand of ones we
trusted the most, a disease that brings our life to a close—these
prayers bring us what we need the most.

THE PRAYER FOR FORGIVENESS

> *Abba,* forgive them; for they know not what they do. (Luke
> 23:34)

Radical forgiveness was central to the message of Jesus. The power of the kingdom was the power to heal and to forgive. The two connect at the deepest of places. This forgiveness came not requiring prior repentance, but rather bringing it. It was extended to all, to those considered unclean and incapable of being cleansed: prostitutes, tax collectors, lepers, sinners, Gentiles.

The forgiveness of sins was central to the disciples' mission as Jesus sent them out into the world. When the risen Christ appeared to the disciples and sent them anew into the world, what he sent them to do began with the words, "If you forgive the sins of any, they are forgiven" (John 20:23).

On the cross, whom was Jesus forgiving? Those closest to him who betrayed him? Yes. The collusion of Roman and Jewish leaders who found it expedient to put him away? Yes. The crowd who went mindlessly along? Yes. These and more.

This prayer forgives us all, for none of us knows the full extent of our sins or the extent of the harm we have done. Albert Speer, one of the leaders of the Third Reich, repented of his involvement in the Nazi regime. As part of the working out of his remorse and repentance he wrote his exposé *Inside the Third Reich*. In a recent book, *Albert Speer: His Battle with the Truth*, the author suggests that for all his truth-telling, Speer was never able to face the complete truth about how early it was that he learned about the Final Solution against the Jews. Was the reason for his incapacity that he at some level believed he could not admit the truth and live?

Jesus' bestowal of forgiveness reaches to us all. Can you hear the sound of Jesus' voice praying for you? It reaches to those places of culpability we acknowledge—and to those places we cannot face in ourselves.

Jesus' prayer on the cross was the beginning of a forgiveness movement that has reached around the world; two thousand years later it is still at work healing the deepest wounds of humanity.

A young Hellenist named Stephen, an early leader of the Christian movement, felt the transformative power of this prayer for forgiveness from the cross. As he was arrested and being stoned to death for his leadership in the movement, Stephen looked up into heaven and prayed two prayers that echo two of

Jesus' prayers from the cross. The first was, "Lord Jesus, receive my spirit." The second was a prayer said aloud for all to hear, "Lord, do not hold this sin against them" (Acts 7:59-60).

Jesus' own prayer from the cross had transformed Stephen's life and now shaped the way he died. In the party of executioners there was a young Pharisee named Saul of Tarsus. It is likely he had orchestrated Stephen's execution. Did Stephen's prayer affect him? Later, now an apostle of the Christ whose followers he had once persecuted, he wrote:

> While we were yet helpless...Christ died for the ungodly.... While we were yet sinners Christ died for us.... While we were enemies we were reconciled to God by the death of his Son. (Romans 5:6-10)

Paul had experienced Jesus' prayer from the cross and Stephen's echo of it, as Christ's prayer for *him*, "*Abba*, forgive them; for they know not what they do."

Jesus' forgiveness movement has carried on, making its impact all over the world. I offer three vignettes of its transformative impact from the twentieth century. The first is an Associated Press photograph.[3] Evidently there has been a Klan rally in Ann Arbor, Michigan. Some anti-Klan protesters have joined the fray and have begun beating a Klan member wearing a Confederate flag.

There in the photograph, a young black woman has intervened. Keshia Thomas, an eighteen-year-old African American, is shielding the racist from those trying to beat him, shielding him with her own body.

There he is, skin-headed, tattooed, with what looks like a racist slur printed on his T-shirt. And there is Keshia, daughter of God, member of the atonement community of Christ, laying her body between him and them.

The second is a story passed down to me about John Lewis, one of the great young leaders of the Civil Rights movement in America, perhaps second only to Martin Luther King, Jr. in stature.

Lewis had been one of the leaders in the first Selma-to-

AP / Wide World Pictures

"There in the photograph, a young black woman has intervened. Keshia Thomas, an eighteen-year old African-American, is shielding the racist from those trying to beat him, shielding him with her own body."

Montgomery march. Governor George Wallace sent his troops to beat the marchers back, which they did with uncontrolled brutality. Lewis had his skull cracked open.

Years later, between terms as governor, Wallace, now in a wheelchair, paralyzed by an assassin's bullet, called John Lewis and asked him to come visit. Lewis did.

Governor Wallace said, "John, I need your forgiveness. Can you find it in your heart to forgive me?" John said, "Yes, Governor, I forgive you." Then Wallace asked: "Do you think God has it in his heart to forgive me?" John replied, "Governor Wallace, I'm even more certain about that." [4]

The last vignette, is a prayer scrawled on a scrap piece of paper by someone killed in the German death camp at Buchenwald:

> O, Lord, when I shall come with glory in your kingdom, do not remember only the men of good will; remember also the men of evil. May they be remembered not only for their acts of cruelty in this camp, the evil they have done to us prisoners, but balance against their cruelty the fruits we have reaped under the stress and in the pain; the comradeship, the courage, the greatness of heart, the humility and patience which have been born in us and become part of our lives, because we have suffered at their hands.... May the memory of us not be a nightmare to them when they stand in judgment. May all that we have suffered be acceptable to you as a ransom for them. [5]

Then at the end, the person quoted these words of Jesus from John's Gospel: "Unless a grain of wheat falls into the earth and dies" (John 12:24). [6]

This is what is saving the world. And it starts with a prayer from the cross, the one Jesus prayed, the one that even now forms our lives.

THE CRY OF DESOLATION

> "Eli, Eli, lama sabach-tha-ni?" that is, My God, my God, why
> hast thou forsaken me? (Matthew 27:46)

It is a cry, a terrible cry, perhaps a cry we all make, if only to
ourselves. It is the cry of meaninglessness when we wonder if anything makes sense, wonder if God is really there, wonder if there
is any reason to keep on living by the values of a God we cannot
see, a God who seems terrifyingly powerless or bewilderingly
absent when the worst happens.

Anne Lamott has a friend who says that sometimes our minds
are like a bad neighborhood we don't want to enter alone. Here is
the gospel: There is no part of our mind we have to enter alone.
Jesus has been there before.

Jesus of Nazareth, who lived in the most extraordinary sense of
God-belovedness, also experienced the darkest of nights, the
night of God-forsakenness. Peter Kreeft writes of the incarnation
of Christ:

> He came. He entered time and space and suffering.
> He came, like a lover. . . . He sits beside us in the low-
> est places of our lives, like water. Are we broken? He
> is broken with us. Are we rejected? . . . He was
> despised and rejected of men. . . . Do we weep? . . . He
> was a "man of sorrows and acquainted with grief." . . .
> Does he descend into all our hells? Yes. In the unfor-
> gettable line of Corrie ten Boom from the depths of
> the Nazi death camp, "No matter how deep our dark-
> ness, he is deeper still."[7]

This cry marks the deepest pitch of darkness. At this moment
he did not know, could not have known, what would happen with
his death, whether there would be any vindication of his life or of
his cause, the kingdom of God, whether his death would be part
of God's redemption of the world, or his life would become one
more nameless body thrown away to rot, whether beyond his last

breath he would land in the arms of God, whether there was anything to this spiritual hope called Resurrection.

He did not know, he could not have known. If Jesus entered
fully into our humanity, he entered fully into our ignorance. His
cry was a real cry: "Eli, Eli, lama sabach-tha-ni? ... my God, my
God, why hast thou forsaken me?"

The book of Hebrews contains in its earliest manuscripts a
phrase that was later changed because it made the church too
uncomfortable. Hebrews 2:9 says, *Choris theou*, "*far from* God he
might taste death for every one." The word *choris*, "far," was
changed to *charis*, "grace." It now reads in most translations, "By
the *grace* of God he might taste death for everyone."

We could not bear the thought of Jesus being far from God, so
we changed the word. But at the moment on the cross, Jesus, who
had been so close to God, experienced being far from God and
cried, "My God, why hast thou forsaken me?"

There is a Jewish commentary on Deuteronomy 3:25, where
Moses cried out to God to let him enter the promised land. It says
that prayer has ten names, and the first name is "Cry."

What can we do with this cry? Is not one of our most primal
fears the fear of forsakenness? Forsakenness by others, by God? It
is woven throughout Scripture. A computer search on the word
"forsaken" turns this up:

> Sixteen times: "God's people have forsaken God."
> Fourteen times: God saying, "If you forsake me, I will forsake
> you."
> Thirteen times: "If you forsake God, God will bring judg-
> ment."
> Twelve times: The promise of God, "I will never leave you or
> forsake you."
> Six times: The plea, "God, do not forsake me, do not hide
> your face from me."
> Three times: The vow, "Lord, we will not forsake you."
> Two times: "The Lord has forsaken us."
> One time: From Psalm 22:1,"My God, my God, why hast
> thou forsaken me?"

One time: From Jesus' lips, "Eli, Eli, lama sabach-tha-ni? . . .
My God, my God, why hast thou forsaken me?"

How deep is our fear of forsakenness! We are dealing with the
profoundest of pain, psychologically and spiritually.

On the cross, Jesus entered even into the experience of God-
forsakenness so that even *there* we will not be alone. He descended
even into the hell of meaninglessness to be with us there and lead
us from that dark prison into the light.

Martin Luther looked at this cry from the cross and sat uncom-
prehendingly before it. "God forsaken of God?" he wrote: "Who
can comprehend it?"

In Bach's masterpiece *The St. Matthew Passion*, whenever the bari-
tone soloist sings Jesus' words, there is a soft "halo" of strings surrounding his words, a musical halo depicting his divinity, all
except when Jesus utters "Eli, Eli, lama sabach-tha-ni?" There the
violins, violas, and cellos are removed. Here was Jesus completely
human, stripped of all divinity.

All life long he lived in the immediacy of God's presence. *"Abba,"*
he called God, with the trust, intimacy, and confidence of a child to
a perfectly loving parent. Now he is willing to suffer godforsakeness
for us, not knowing whether this night would ever turn to day.

There are those who try to soften the agony of the cry by saying, he is quoting Psalm 22, and Psalm 22 ends with an exclama-
tion of trust. By quoting verse 1, they say, he was referring to all
the verses of the psalm. This may well have been the *faith* of Jesus
at that moment; but it was *faith*, not *knowledge*. At that moment he
did not know, could not have known.

Tillich seeks to underline the unbroken trust of Jesus at that
moment by saying that Jesus still cried, "My God, my God." But
at that moment Jesus did not know, could not have known. He
walked by faith, not by sight (as we all must)—by faith, without
the props of feeling or proof or spiritual experience.

In Psalm 22 the psalmist cries, "I am a worm, and no man."
There are moments in life we can be reduced, feel reduced, to
something less than human.

I remember a Sunday morning in Louisville with a man about my

age named David. He was a decorated Vietnam veteran, a helicop-
ter pilot. He had suffered, as the other soldiers of that war, not only
the terrors and traumas of war but the trauma of coming home from
that war to a nation who would not welcome him home because it
was so divided about the war. Thirty years after the end of the war
we held a Sunday morning worship service for Vietnam veterans.
We were seeking to provide a spiritual homecoming for soldiers and
some kind of healing for us all so deeply hurt by that war.

Our church had been a leader in peace and justice work in
Louisville. We had sponsored peace conferences. We had invited
a controversial Jesuit priest to speak. But we were a community of
reconciliation, and we wanted also to honor the soldiers who had
done their duty to their nation and had incurred great suffering in
the process.

The day before the worship service we had gone to the
Veterans' Day festivities downtown to give out flyers inviting
everyone to the worship service and Sunday dinner. There you
saw the most amazing collection of humanity: men on Harleys
and men in wheelchairs, men maimed in body and soul, some with
long hair and tattoos, others crew cut and in uniform, all bearing
scars of one kind or another from the war.

We asked David to take part in the service and if he wished, to
wear his uniform. He came in uniform, bearing his medals, the
first time they had been out of the box in thirty years, he said.

Before the service we walked past the communion table. He
pointed me to the open Bible on the table. It lay open to Psalm
31. He pointed to verse 11. I read the words:

I am the scorn of all my adversaries,
a horror to my neighbors,
an object of dread to my acquaintances;
those who see me in the street flee from me.
I have passed out of mind like one who is dead;
I have become like a broken vessel.

That's how he felt; he had felt that for thirty years. After the service and after the church dinner that followed, he said, with tears

running down his cheeks, "I've been waiting thirty years for this."

I learned last year that a few years ago he committed suicide. Since the Vietnam War ended, more soldiers have died prematurely than died in the war itself. Perhaps he never quite escaped the darkness of Psalm 31.

But I hope and I pray that somewhere in the darkness he met the one who cried, "My God, my God, why hast thou forsaken me?" and that Jesus led him all the way home to God.

We have in Jesus a Savior who has come all the way, endured everything, to meet us in the darkest possible night and lead us to day. It may be pitch black. The night may last far longer than you are able to fathom. But there's a hand there in the darkness, the hand of one who knows the heights of God-belovedness and the depths of God-forsakenness, one who cried, "Eli, Eli, lama sabach-tha-ni?" and who has descended into hell to take your hand.

There are days we are not so much interested in the question, "Is there life after death?" as the question, "Is there life after hell?"—the hell we are experiencing here.

I do not know a greater darkness than the darkness of forsakenness, of despair, of loss of meaning, of being cut off from others and from God. Jesus has gone even there, endured even that, so that even there he will be with us, take our hand, and lead us from that dark prison into freedom and into the light.

First Peter 3:19 says in an often debated passage that at his death Jesus entered into the realm of the dead and preached to the spirits in prison, leading them from darkness and death to light and life. He is preaching still, through this cry.

THE RELINQUISHMENT

Abba, into thy hands I commit my spirit! (Luke 23:46)

With this last prayer, Jesus releases himself into the hands of God. He begins as he began all his prayers, except the cry of desolation, with the word *Abba.* His life was carried from beginning to end by his *Abba*-experience of God, his sense of God's loving presence, his trust in the goodness of God.

"*Abba*," he cried in joy as a boy romping through fields strewn with wildflowers.

"*Abba*" was who he sought in the temple when he was twelve years old, so absorbed that he missed his family's departure from Jerusalem. He was about his *Abba's* business, he told his exasperated parents.

"*Abba*," he taught us to pray, "our *Abba* in heaven."

"*Abba*, I thank you," he prayed when he realized the tide had turned against him, when he knew his own people and the religious establishment had turned on him and that those who were following him were outcasts, sinners, women, children, and assorted Gentiles.

"*Abba*," he cried in the garden, hoping to be spared the cross. And now, on the cross he cries, "*Abba*, into thy hands I commit my spirit." Does this contradict his other cry? "Eli, Eli, lama sabachtha-ni? . . . My God, my God why hast thou forsaken me?" Yes and no. It is the opposite human emotion. But to be human means to have opposite emotions. And to *feel* forsaken does not mean to *be* forsaken.

When Jesus says, "Into thy hands I commit my spirit," he is quoting Psalm 31, the psalm the Vietnam veteran pointed out to me that Sunday:

> In thee, O LORD, do I seek refuge;
> let me never be put to shame. . . .
> I am the scorn of all my adversaries,
> a horror to my neighbors. . . .
> I have become like a broken vessel. (vv. 1, 11, 12)

In the midst of all this the psalmist says, "Into thy hand I commit my spirit" (Psalm 31:5). Into thy hand I commit my *ruach*, my breath, my spirit, my life. It is a phrase to live by and to die by: O God, into thy hand I offer all I am and all I have and all I love.

It is the spiritual movement of "letting go." We say, "O God, I take my sticky fingers off the controls and place my life in better hands than mine." It is what Catherine Marshall called "the prayer of relinquishment," which is what we all someday must pray as we hold what is dearest in our hands.

I like John Ruskin's words about an artist finishing a painting. He or she never does finish, not perfectly. The painting is finished by God, in God. "God alone can finish." We do our best, then let it go.

Reinhold Niebuhr wrote these words about how our work, our lives fit in the larger scheme of things;

> Nothing that is worth doing can be achieved in a lifetime; therefore we must be saved by hope. Nothing which is true or beautiful or good makes complete sense in any immediate context of history; therefore we must be saved by faith. Nothing we do, however virtuous, can be accomplished alone. Therefore we are saved by love.[8]

"O God," we pray, "I've done what I could. Finish this work, 'into thy hands.' "

Psalm 31 is an "evening psalm" in Hebrew tradition. I have heard that this verse that Jesus quoted, "Into thy hands I commit my spirit," was the nighttime prayer of Jewish boys and girls. It is kin to our "Now I lay me down to sleep," "*Abba*, into thy hands. . . ."

I do not know whether this is so. But could we go to sleep or wake from sleep with better words? Into thy hands I commit my spirit, my life, my efforts, all I have and all I love. *Abba*, into thy hands. Here is faith at its most basic: We live and die, wake and sleep, love and work in the Lord, by the hand of the One who is making all things well. These are Jesus' prayers from the cross. They are the best words we can say when life presents its crosses to us.

CHAPTER 7

Prayers from John:
That We May Be One

J ohn's Gospel has been called the "spiritual Gospel" and "the mystical Gospel." In Christian iconography, the symbol for the Fourth Gospel is the eagle. It soars, and it comes near an almost blinding light.

John's Gospel is different from the three synoptic Gospels, Matthew, Mark, and Luke. They, as the word "synoptic" suggests, see the life of Jesus with "one eye." John's Gospel looks with another.

John's Gospel is different in chronology, in an early Judean ministry, in long spiritual and philosophical discourses, and in Jesus' astounding claims: "Before Abraham was, I am," "I am the way, and the truth, and the life," "I and the Father are one" (8:58, 14:6, 10:30). Only John's Gospel has Jesus and his disciples baptizing (and that didn't appear to last long). Only in John does Jesus celebrate *three* Passovers, which has given us the hint that his ministry lasted three years.

John emphasizes a mystical union between Jesus and God— and a mystical union possible between the human and the divine. So it seems most appropriate that the main prayer of Jesus has as its central petition:

Holy *Abba*, keep them in your name
which you have given to me,

that they may be one,
even as we are one. (17:11*b* RSV, adapted)

John speaks of the Incarnation as the *logos*, the eternal Word of God, becoming flesh and "dwelling" among us. Jesus speaks of his abiding in us and our abiding in him.

In the synoptic Gospels, the main metaphor of Jesus' preaching is "the kingdom of God." In John, the main metaphor is entering into *zoe*, life, a full, abundant, everlasting life. There is a birthing from above, by the Spirit, a being "born anew" that is our entrance into such life. And what the New Testament scholar C. H. Dodd famously called "realized eschatology" can begin *now*.

In John, organic images are used to symbolize this *zoe*, this union with God: vine and branches, living water welling up from within. Jesus is both "light" and "life." An early Christian pictograph used those two words to fashion a cross and symbolize Christianity: *phos* (light) and *zoe* (life):

In John's Gospel the words of the risen Christ through the Spirit seem as important as the words of the historical Jesus.[1] We see the pithy sayings of Jesus recorded in the synoptic Gospels expanded into long spiritual discourses in John. After all, Jesus had told them that the Holy Spirit, the *Paraclete*, would continue to teach them when he, Jesus, had gone (John 14:25-26).

There are three prayers of Jesus in John's Gospel. One is the Johannine parallel to Jesus' Gethsemane prayer:

Now my soul is troubled.
And what shall I say, "*Abba*, save me from this hour"?
No, for this purpose I have come to this hour.
Abba, glorify your name. (John 12:27 RSV, adapted)

John's version shows a Jesus less shaken, more resolute than in Mark's Gethsemane prayer. The struggle is there, but more muted. Jesus seems to have already turned the corner from a soul in agony to a soul ready to relinquish itself into God's purpose and God's hands.

His prayer, "for this purpose I have come to this hour," echoes the Gethsemane words, "Not what I want, but what you want"; and the words of the Lord's Prayer, "Your kingdom come. Your will be done." His cry, "*Abba*, glorify your name," echoes the petition of the Lord's Prayer, "Hallowed be your name."

As Jesus prays facing his own death, I am reminded of the poem of Dietrich Bonhoeffer, "Who am I?" written while in prison facing execution by order of Hitler. "Am I the heroic figure others see me to be," he asked, "or the frightened weakling I know myself at times to be?" He ends the poem:

> Who am I? They mock me, these lonely questions of
>   mine.
> Whoever I am, Thou knowest, O God, I am Thine! [2]

The second prayer of Jesus is prayed at Lazarus's tomb. Lazarus, his close friend, has died. Jesus is about to call on the power of God to raise him from the tomb. He "looks upward," the first century posture of prayer, and prays:

> *Abba*, I thank you that you have heard me. I know that you always hear me. (John 11:41 NRSV, adapted)

We glimpse again the extraordinary intimacy Jesus felt with God. God was always listening, always close by, and always ready to help. "I know that you always hear me." It is with this same confidence Jesus invited his disciples, and invites us, to pray. God's ear is always inclined to us.

In John 9:31, the religious leaders state the conventional theology of prayer: "We know that God pays no attention to sinners, but He does listen to someone who is devout and obeys His will." [3] Jesus believed quite the opposite. God hears everyone's prayers,

perhaps especially the prayers of sinners because they are more apt
to pray to God and less apt to make speeches to God. (See Jesus'
parable of the Pharisee and the Tax Collector, Luke 18:10-14.)

Now comes the second phrase of the prayer, one that may give
us pause:

> But I have said this because of the crowd standing here,
> that they may believe that you sent me. (John 11:42 NRSV,
> adapted)

Some scholars have been taken aback by what appears to them
to be a prayer prayed not primarily to God but to the "gallery" in
order to impress them.[4] But nothing could be farther from the
spirit of Jesus or from his teaching on prayer: "When you pray, go
into your room and shut the door and pray to your Father who is
in secret" (Matthew 6:6).

However, the words "I have said this" refer not so much to the
prayer itself as to the prior words in verse 40: "Did I not tell you
that if you believed you would see the glory of God?"

The prayer of Jesus is prayed to *God*, and it is as if they are the
only two in the room. They now abide in one another. Here is a
prayer of praise and thanksgiving. Jesus trusts that God is about to
reveal the divine glory by the raising of Lazarus.

In John, the miracles are called "signs," and they are done to
help people believe. "Faith" is a verb in John, a trusting in God.
Jesus gives thanks to God and prays that the sign will lead people
to believe. He is here like the Hebrew prophet Elijah on Mt.
Carmel praying for a miracle:

> Answer me, O LORD, answer me, that this people may know
> that thou, O LORD, art God, and that thou hast turned their
> hearts back. (1 Kings 18:37)

This prayer, then, is not spiritual grandstanding. It is ecstatic
prayer, flowing thanks. And it voices the petition that we will be
able to see the glory of God in our midst and believe.

The third prayer is the focus for this chapter. The prayer comprises all twenty-six verses of chapter 17. It is often called the "high priestly prayer," an apt title, for the priest is the one trying to bring heaven to earth and earth to heaven, seeking somehow to be a bridge where the meeting of God and humanity can take place. The prayer is the close of a longer "farewell speech" (13:31–17:26), a final message to his disciples, and it ends much like Moses' final discourse to the children of Israel, with a prayer of petition and a prayer of blessing.[5]

I focus on one verse, that I take to be the centerpiece of the long prayer:

> Holy *Abba*, keep them in your name
> which you have given to me,
> that they may be one,
> even as we are one. (17:11*b* RSV, adapted)

"Holy *Abba*," he began, a phrase that echoes the whole line of the Lord's Prayer, "Our *Abba* in heaven, hallowed be your name."

Jesus prays, "Keep them in your name." Keep them in relationship, relationship as close as the giving and receiving of names. And the name? *Yahweh*, yes, the divine name given Israel, and now *Abba*.

Who is the "them" for whom Jesus prayed? His disciples there with him, yes. But the prayer was also for all those who would become his disciples because of the witness of that first circle of disciples, "I do not pray for these only, but also for those who are to believe in me through their word, that they may all be one" (John 17:20).

The circle of those who will be part of the Shepherd's flock is wider than we know. In John 10, Jesus said:

> I am the good shepherd; I know my own and my own know me ... and I lay down my life for the sheep. *And I have other sheep, that are not of this fold;* I must bring them also, and they will heed my voice. So there shall be one flock, one shepherd. (John 10:14-16, emphasis mine)

Those words should cheer us. Some days we all wonder whether we are in the fold. There are more persons on the way with Christ than we can imagine.

There is an astonishing assurance given to those who find themselves in the flock of God. We may feel weak or stupid, overwhelmed by the powers that seek to destroy us and God's world, powers that try to separate us from God. But listen to Jesus' next words:

> My sheep hear my voice, and I know them, and they follow me; and I give them eternal life [*zoen aionion*, a life forever] and they shall never perish [*apolontai eis ton aiona*, shall not perish forever], and no one shall snatch them out of my hand. My Father, who has given them to me, is greater than all, and no one is able to snatch them out of the Father's hand. I and the Father are one. (John 10:27-30)

Some people bristle at the phrase "I and the Father are one." It sounds presumptuous or exclusive. Like Jesus was claiming too much for himself—or that John was claiming too much for Jesus. But we misread it because we read it through creedal formulations made four centuries later, and because we've seen it used by Christians as a hammer of superiority, as a card to trump other religious faiths.

The "oneness" of which Jesus spoke was inherent in the intimacy and trust of his prayer to *Abba*, and his experience of God as *Abba*. It is the oneness of relation.

Moreover Jesus prayed that *you and I* be one just as he and God were one. Here is oneness not as a claim of spiritual superiority, but oneness meant for all, oneness in spirit, oneness in love, oneness in beloved community, oneness in life, spiritual, abundant, eternal life.

This oneness is not the possession of Christianity. It is the gift of God to all the world: Christian, Muslim, Jew, Buddhist, Hindu, and Druid. And to people who have no faith to speak of because the "faith" they have been presented is too small, too twisted, too smug, too mean.

This prayer of Jesus is the oneness of earthly redemption Jesus called the "kingdom of God" and of the cosmic redemption Paul called "the new creation."

This prayer of Jesus peers toward Easter. It is as though Jesus were already on his ascent to the cross and then to God's eternal glory. Easter is God's encircling yes, the visible dawn of God's love for all. Easter then, belongs to the world, not to the church. It is a gift given to the church, but is not its possession. It belongs to the cry of justice, to the longing for cease-fire and peace, it belongs to those who are oppressed and long to be free, it belongs to the dying, and it belongs to those being made new.

The oneness of God with us is a oneness of *being*. We were created in the image of God, male and female. In the Spirit of God, we experience this oneness as children of God.

The oneness of God with us is the oneness of *moral purpose*. A friend is one who takes up your cause. So we take up God's cause in the world. Jesus said, "If you keep my commandments, you will abide in my love, just as I have kept my Father's commandments and abide in his love" (John 15:10). And the greatest commandment? "This is my commandment, that you love one another as I have loved you" (John 15:12).

And there is the oneness of *mutual indwelling*, what the mystics call a "unitive experience" where the boundaries between God and us fall away and we are at one with God and with God's creation. Thomas Merton experienced such a unitive experience one day while standing on a city street:

> In Louisville, at the corner of Fourth and Walnut, in the center of the shopping district, I was suddenly overwhelmed with the realization that I loved all those people, that they were mine and I theirs, that we could not be alien to one another even though we were total strangers.... I have the immense joy of being a [human person], a member of a race in which God Himself became incarnate. As if the sorrows and stupidities of the human condition could overwhelm me, now I realize what we all are. And if only

everybody could realize this! But it cannot be
explained. There is no way of telling people that they
are all walking around shining like the sun. [6]

Julian of Norwich, the fourteenth-century British anchorite and
mystic, was given "revelations" or "showings" by God. It was May
8, 1373. The most famous of the lines given her was God's
promise:

> All shall be well
> and all shall be well,
> all manner of things
> shall be well.

Here is the twelfth revelation, shown first in medieval English and
with her idiosyncratic spelling:

> I it am, I it am;
> I it am that is heyest;
> I it am that thou lovist;
> I it am that thou lykst;
> I it am that thou servist;
> I it am that thou longyst;
> I it am that thou desyrist;
> I it am that thou menyst;
> I it am that is al;
> I it am that holy church prechyth and teachyth the;
> I it am that shewed me here to thee. [7]

And now in my (more) modern rendering.

> It is I, It is I;
> It is I that is highest;
> It is I that thou lovest;
> It is I that thou likest;
> It is I that thou servest;
> It is I of your longing;
> It is I whom you desire;
> I am what you mean;

It is I that is all;
It is I the holy church preaches and teaches you;
It is I that showed me here to you.

The oneness for which Jesus prayed on our behalf was the over-coming of the separateness or estrangement we feel in relation to God, self, others, and life itself.

Some people seem to live life with a basic sense of oneness with God, with a deep sense of blessing and well-being. Such grace seems to have come as a gift of creation itself. These are those William James called "once-born" in his seminal psychology of religion *The Varieties of Religious Experience.* [8] Such people cannot remember a time when they did not know themselves a Christian or a child of God. It is as if they have breathed the Spirit of God with their natural breath from day one. When they took their first breath, God's breath was there. Conversion for the "once-born" is not some dramatic cataclysmic turnaround as much as the gradual growth of one who is growing in the love of God and neighbor, as a flower turns its face almost imperceptibly toward the sun.

In contrast, the "twice-born" person, to use William James's distinction, seems to have lived always with a division of soul, or divided self. They experience to an almost excruciating degree the *distance* between themselves and God, the *difference* between themselves and God. They keenly feel the struggle within between good and evil. They sharply perceive the struggle between good and evil in the world around them. They have an acute, sometimes morbidly active conscience.

Their predominant spiritual experience is not oneness with God and the world but rather estrangement and alienation. Conversion often comes for the "twice-born" when by some dramatic turn they move from estrangement to union, from alienation to oneness, from divided self to a wholeness and wellness of being. The apostle Paul was no doubt a "twice-born" Christian. Flannery O'Connor said of him, "I reckon the Lord knew that the only way to make a Christian out of that one was to knock him off his horse." [9]

Both "once-born" and "twice-born" persons are children of God with their own spiritual journeys to make. Our contemporary brain science is suggesting a neurological connection to mystical experience. The part of the brain that helps us define the boundaries between self and the world alters its activity when a person has an experience of oneness with God and with all life. One study tracks brain activity for Franciscan nuns at prayer and Buddhist monks in contemplation. [10] Perhaps some are more neurologically wired for the unitive experience, but particular forms of "spiritual practice" may help us all have such experiences.

Erik Erikson's seminal psychological work suggests that early experience can shape one's basic sense of trust or mistrust. Traumatic life experiences or the experience of moral transgression may bring a profound experience of being estranged. Whatever the causes and conditions, God seeks the movement from alienation to restoration, from estrangement to oneness, from dis-ease to peace.

Jesus prays for us all, the once-born or the twice-born, the blessed and the anguished, the ones who have strayed destructively from the path of God and *zoe* and those who haven't, that we may all be one even as Jesus and God were one.

Such is the meaning of the "new birth," of being "born from above," anew, by the Spirit (John 3). And such a part is the meaning of what Paul called the "new creation": "So if anyone is in Christ, there is a new creation!" (2 Corinthians 5:17 NRSV). The old translations went: "If anyone is in Christ, he is a new creature." But this "new creation" is more than personal transformation. It is cosmic in scope. It is more than what is happening in us; it includes what is going on in all creation.

> The old is gone, look, the new has come! All this is from God, who through Christ reconciled us to God's own self and has given to us the ministry [*diakonia*] of reconciliation. (2 Corinthians 5:17-18 AT)

Oneness is reconciliation after so long a journey apart. It is the "new creation" invading the old order of things and remaking it. [11] Oneness is not only gift, it is also calling, a *diakonia*, a ministry. It is the announcing of the new—God's new creation transforming the present age and overcoming all that is oppressive and dehumanizing. And we are the followers of Jesus, we are the heralds of this "new creation" through our service, our *diakonia*, to the world.

In Parker Palmer's book *The Active Life: A Spirituality of Work, Creativity and Caring*,[12] Palmer reflects on the meaning of vocation and quotes these words by Joseph Campbell:

> People say that what we're all seeking is a meaning for life. I don't think that's what we're really seeking. I think that what we are seeking is an experience of being alive, so that our life experiences on the purely physical plane will have resonances with our innermost being and reality, so that we actually feel the rapture of being alive.

Parker modifies Campbell and goes one more step. He writes:

> For me, the heart of the spiritual quest is to know "the rapture of being alive," and (here is where I find Campbell incomplete) to allow that knowledge to transform us into celebrants, advocates, defenders of life wherever we find it.[13]

To be only interested in the "rapture of being alive" would make us endlessly self-absorbed, but to connect that rapture with God's great work of justice, love, and peace, is our calling. It is the calling of reconciliation: That we all may be one. In *diakonia* our oneness with God is making us partners with God in the saving work of reconciliation.

"You must be born anew, born again, from above," Jesus said to Nicodemus (John 3:7 RSV, adapted). "I came that they may have life, and have it abundantly," this Jesus said—*zoe*, life eternal, life abundant, life forever (John 10:10). It is joyful, connected, passionate, rapturous life. It is life-in-relation—in right relation with God, with others, with creation, and with your own true self. "That they may be one," Jesus prayed for us, "even as we are one." Such oneness is God's gift and our calling.

The Risen Christ
Returns to Bless

I n the great cathedral art of Christianity, one often sees the figure of the risen Christ, his hands raised in the sign of blessing.
The experience of Easter is of a risen Jesus who returns to his
disciples. The words he said and the prayers he prayed as he met
them were the words and prayers of blessing. One early Easter
antiphon remembers these first words: "Peace be with you, it is I,
alleluia: be not afraid, alleluia."[1]

He did not return to haunt his disciples who had in one way or
another all failed him in his last days, but rather to bless them—to
forgive them and to call them anew. Their response has been ours
throughout the centuries—awed gratitude.

In John's Gospel Jesus appeared first to one of his women disciples, Mary Magdalene. (Jesus had a symbolic circle of twelve
male disciples, called the Twelve, but there was a larger circle of
disciples among whom Mary was prominent.)[2] Upon this
encounter with the risen Jesus, Mary ran to tell the disciples, "I
have seen the Lord." Thus she became known as "apostle to the
apostles,"[3] the first evangelist of the resurrection.

That Easter Sunday evening, he appeared to his disciples who
were huddled in fear behind locked doors. With their leader executed the preceding Friday, they had many reasons to be afraid.

Jesus suddenly appeared to them in the room. The form of his appearance can only be obliquely, paradoxically, described as a "resurrection body." It was not a resuscitated corpse, nor was it merely a ghostlike apparition.

His first words to them were "Peace to you. *Shalom.*" *Shalom* was the bestowal of forgiveness, the renewal of relationship, the gift of healing, wholeness, well-being in all its dimensions—in relation to God and others and inside our own skin.

A second time he said it: "Peace be with you." (Was the first time not enough?) Then he called them anew: "As the Father has sent [apostled] me, so send I you." He was sending them, sending us, to *be* him in the world. They, as we would be, were incredulous, *How could this be?*

Then the text says, he "breathed on them" and said to them, "Receive the Holy Spirit." He described to them the heart of their mission: "If you forgive the sins of any, they will be forgiven." Literally the Greek says: If you *loose* people of their sins, they will be *loosed.* The source of their power to forgive was in the gift of the Spirit, that the Risen One breathed on them—and now breathes on us.

The apostle Paul said that God has sent the Spirit into us, God's children, so that we might cry out *Abba* and pray as Jesus prayed. Through the Spirit we have the "*Abba*-experience" that Jesus had.

With this Spirit and with this experience, we now are sent, apostled, as Jesus was sent, to forgive, to loose people of their sins. We become members of Jesus' forgiveness community, an atonement community that is an "at-one-ment" community. Jesus' return to us in the Resurrection is utter gift, it is full forgiveness, it is life-bestowing.

Luke's Gospel records at its end that Jesus' last words before he ascended into heaven were the words and gesture of blessing:

> Then he led them out as far as Bethany, and lifting up his hands he blessed them. (Luke 24:50)

His last and ongoing prayer is for *his community*, for our wholeness and well-being, and for our vocation in the atonement community of Christ.

He is still at the work of blessing, healing, saving today. I offer one person's story that is deeply moving to me, that of Anne Lamott, a brilliant novelist and writer who lives on the West Coast. God's elusive spirit had been part of her life always, but she had careened from one catastrophe to another.

Somehow she found (or God found for her) a little ghetto church in Marin County across from a flea market. "It is where I was taken in when I had nothing to give," she writes, "and it has become in the truest and deepest sense, my home. My home base." She knew her "wonderful brilliant left-wing friends" would look askance at her love of Jesus.

The encounter with Jesus took place in her houseboat, where she was home recovering from an abortion. She was weak from loss of blood and in a kind of haze produced by a combination of pain medication and whiskey. She suddenly sensed his presence in the room, sitting in the corner of the room "watching with patience and love." She turned away from him to the wall and said out loud, "I would rather die." She fell asleep, and in the morning he was gone.

The next day she wondered whether it was a hallucination "born of fear and self-loathing and booze and the loss of blood."[4] But this Jesus, she writes, "was relentless":

> I didn't experience him so much as the hound of heaven, as the old description has it, as the alley cat of heaven who seemed to believe that if it just keeps showing up, mewling outside your door, you'd eventually open up and give him a bowl of milk. [5]

She resisted until a week or so later when she returned to her church, which had become God's salvation to her. "That's where I was when I came to," she writes, "and there I came to believe." [6]

In church that day, the sermon seemed to her about as sensible as someone trying to convince her of the existence of extraterrestrials. But the last song in worship did it:

> The last song was so deep and raw and pure that I could not escape. It was as if the people were singing in between the notes, weeping and joyful at the same

time, and I felt like their voices or *something* was rock-
ing me in its bosom, holding me like a scared kid, and
I opened up to that feeling—and it washed over me. [7]

She began to cry and left before the benediction. As she raced
home, she sensed Christ, like a little cat, running along at her
heels.

When she arrived at her houseboat, she paused, opened the
door and said to Christ, "I quit.... All right. You can come in."
This, she writes, "was my beautiful moment of conversion."

It was a kind of surrender, but neither she nor we much like the
word "surrender." It feels, she says, like somebody on the play-
ground twisting our arm, rubbing our face in the dirt and saying,
"Give up? Say 'Give!' " A better word, she says, is "yield," which
means, agriculturally speaking, "step aside and let something
grow." Maybe that's the call of Easter faith: Step aside and let
something grow!

Anne Lamott's experience of the living Christ is more dramati-
cally vivid than most people's experience, but it describes the
stunning gratuity of what resurrection is for us all: *Jesus' return to us
in the Resurrection is utter gift, it is full forgiveness, it is life-bestowing.*

The prayers of the risen Jesus were and are prayers of blessing,
prayers of *Shalom* and peace, and prayers that bestow us with the
spirit of life and send us forth to give that life to others.

His prayers, all nine of them, are ways we breathe with Jesus,
breathe in his spirit and live his life on this earth. They are, to use
the novelist Anne Tyler's words, "breathing lessons."

OK, now breathe, breathe deeply. Take in the Spirit of God.
Let its grace and truth flow to every part of your life. Let it oxy-
genate every cell. Let it reform your mind. Let it give you a new
heart. Let your heart beat with the heart of the world, which is
God's own beating heart. It sounds like this:

> Our *Abba* in heaven
> hallowed be your name.
> Your kingdom come,
> your will be done on earth as in heaven.

Give us today our daily bread.
Forgive our sins
as we forgive those who sin against us.
Save us in the time of trial
and deliver us from evil.
For yours is the kingdom
and the power and the glory
now and forever.
Amen.

Notes

PROLOGUE: THE PRAYERS OF JESUS AND THE STORY OF JESUS

1. I am interested in the work of Marcus Borg who has described Jesus' ministry as a "politics of compassion" that confronted and transformed the prevailing "politics of holiness." See *Jesus: A New Vision* (San Francisco: Harper & Row, 1987), pp. 86, 130; and *Meeting Jesus Again for the First Time* (San Francisco: HarperSanFrancisco, 1994), pp. 46-68.

INTRODUCTION: SETTING THE STAGE

1. Joachim Jeremias, *New Testament Theology* (New York: Charles Scribner's Sons, 1971), pp. 36, 178-203.

2. Ann Ulanov and Barry Ulanov, *Primary Speech: A Psychology of Prayer* (Atlanta: John Knox Press, 1982).

3. Ray Kelleher, "Kathleen Norris," *Poets and Writers Magazine*, 25, no. 3 (May/June 1997): 71.

4. E. F. Scott, *The Lord's Prayer* (New York: Scribner, 1951), p. 55.

5. Bruce Wilkinson, *The Prayer of Jabez* (Sisters, Ore.: Multnomah, 2000).

6. The "Jesus Seminar" offers perhaps the most radical conclusions in current New Testament scholarship. See Robert Funk and Roy

Hoover, *The Five Gospels: The Search for the Authentic Words of Jesus* (New York: Macmillan, 1993). The seminar has produced its own translation of the Gospels, printing the words of Jesus in four different colors that represent their judgment on the reliability of Jesus' words. Red signifies that Jesus undoubtedly said this, or something very close to it. Pink signifies that Jesus probably said something like this. Gray signified that Jesus did not say this, but the ideas contained in the words are close to his own. Bold black signifies that Jesus did not say this and that it represents the perspective of a later tradition.

For a sample of current Jesus scholarship, I would recommend the following: Marcus Borg and N. T. Wright, *The Meaning of Jesus: Two Visions* (San Francisco: Harper San Francisco, 1999); John Dominic Crossan, *Jesus: A Revolutionary Biography* (San Francisco: Harper San Francisco, 1994); John P. Meier, *A Marginal Jew: Rethinking the Historical Jesus*, 3 vols. (New York: Doubleday, 1991–2001); Ben Meyer, "Jesus Christ" in *The Anchor Bible Dictionary*, ed. D. Friedman (New York: Doubleday, 1992).

7. See "Abba as an Address to God" in *New Testament Theology*, pp. 61-68.

8. This version of the Lord's Prayer adapts the version used by the *United Methodist Hymnal* (Nashville: United Methodist Publishing House, 1989), #894. This version not only makes good use of current scholarship, but also reacquaints us with its power and truth by the strangeness of its sound and words.

9. George A. Buttrick, *Prayer* (New York: Abingdon Press, 1942), p. 83. For a scholarly estimate of the "Search for the Historical Jesus" and how its conclusions can be influenced by our presuppositions see Helmut Koester, "Jesus the Victim" in *Journal of Biblical Literature* 3, no. 1 (1992): 3-15.

10. Walter Brueggemann, *Ichabod Toward Home: The Journey of God's Glory* (Grand Rapids: Wm. B. Eerdmans, 2002), pp. 88 and 110.

11. J. Louis Martyn, "An Open Letter to the Biblical Guild about Liberation" (unpublished essay, 1972).

1. JESUS AND PRAYER

1. Joachim Jeremias, *New Testament Theology* (New York: Charles Scribner's Sons, 1971), p. 63.

2. See *Didache* 8:3. The *Didache* was the earliest church manual, dating from late-first century to mid-second century.

3. *New Testament Theology*, p. 185.

4. Cited in Lucien Deiss, *Springtime of the Liturgy: Liturgical Texts of the First Four Centuries* (Collegeville, -Minn.: The Liturgical Press, 1979), pp. 7-8.

5. Ibid., p. 17.

6. Bernard Brandon Scott, *Hear Then the Parable* (Minneapolis: Fortress Press, 1989), p. 88.

7. *New Testament Theology*, p. 186.

2. THE LORD'S PRAYER, PART 1

1. Gerd Theissen, *The Shadow of the Galilean: The Quest for the Historical Jesus in Narrative Form* (Philadelphia: Fortress Press, 1986), pp. 68-71, 148, 210.

2. See John Howard Yoder, *The Politics of Jesus* (Grand Rapids: Wm. B. Eerdmans, 1972), pp. 26-77.

3. Lucien Deiss, *Springtime of the Liturgy: Liturgical Texts of the First Four Centuries* (Collegeville, Minn.: The Liturgical Press, 1979), p. 19.

4. I am indebted to Kenneth Stevenson for this description of the shape of the Lord's Prayer. See his excellent *Abba Father: Understanding and Using the Lord's Prayer* (Harrisburg, Penn.: Morehouse, 2000), pp. 34-35.

5. Tertullian, "De Oratione I," *The Ante-Nicene Fathers*, eds. Alexander Roberts and James Donaldson (Edinburgh: T & T Clark, 1993), p. 681.

6. Joachim Jeremias, *New Testament Theology* (New York: Charles Scribner's Sons, 1971), p. 186.

7. Ibid., p. 66. See also his *Prayers of Jesus* (Napierville, Ill.: Alec R. Allenson, 1967).

8. Current scholarship has challenged Jeremias successfully on several points. They have substantiated the use of *Abba* as a name for God and an address to God in the Judaism of that historical period. They

have shown that Jeremias's early tendency to make *Abba* a child's word and to emphasize its intimate and familiar tone ("Daddy" or "Poppa") is overdrawn. They have noted that his tendency to accentuate the difference between Jesus and Judaism made him a child of his time and culture, which worked to deemphasize Jesus' Jewishness.

To sample the scholarly critique of Jeremias, I recommend two articles. The first is James Barr, "Abba Isn't 'Daddy,'" *Journal of Theological Studies*, 39, no. 1 (April 1988): 28-47, a brilliant philological study of Jesus' use of *Abba*. The second is Mary Rose DeAngelo, "Abba and Father: Imperial Theology and the Jesus Tradition," *Journal of Biblical Literature*, 3, no. 4 (1992): 611-30, a more critical repudiation of Jeremias's thesis. It also considers how *Abba* and "pater" functioned as a critique of the Roman imperial theology: God is king and father, not Caesar.

9. James D. G. Dunn, *Jesus and the Spirit* (London: SCM Press, 1975), p. 21.

10. See "Abba Isn't 'Daddy'" and "Abba and Father: Imperial Theology and the Jesus Tradition," cited above.

11. James Barr, "Abba Isn't 'Daddy,' " *Journal of Theological Studies* 39, no. 1 (April 1988): 44-45.

12. Martin Buber, *Modern Man and the Jewish Bible*, as cited on the Martin Buber homepage, www.buber.de/en/index.html.

13. Gail Ramshaw, *Reviving Sacred Speech: The Meaning of Liturgical Language* (Akron, Ohio: DSL Publications, 2000), p. 64.

14. Brennan Manning, *Abba's Child: The Cry of the Heart for Intimate Belonging* (Colorado Springs: Navpress, 1994), p. 64.

3. THE LORD'S PRAYER, PART 2

1. Mary Oliver, "The Summer Day," *New and Selected Poems* (Boston: Beacon Press, 1992), p. 94.

2. Wendell Berry, "Two Economies" in *The Art of the Commonplace* (Washington, D.C.: Counterpoint, 2002), p. 220.

3. *Love and Anger: Song of Lively Faith and Social Justice* (Iona Community: Wild Goose Worship Group, 1998).

4. C. S. Lewis, *Letters to Malcolm: Chiefly on Prayer* (New York: Brace & World, 1963), p. 106.

5. Kenneth Stevenson, *Abba Father: Understanding and Using the Lord's Prayer* (Harrisburg, Penn.: Morehouse, 2000), p. 108.

6. C. S. Lewis, *Surprised by Joy* (New York: Harcourt Brace & Company, 1955), p. 226.

4. PRAYER AMID LIFE'S REVERSALS

1. My paraphrase of Rainer Maria Rilke, sonnet 1.7, *Sonnets to Orpheus*, trans. David Young (Hanover, N.H.: Wesleyan University Press, 1987), p. 15. Young's translation goes: "Praising, that's it! / Praise was his mission."

2. Denise Levertov, "Poetry, Prophecy, Survival," in *New and Selected Essays* (New York: New Directions, 1992), p. 144.

3. Edward Hirsch, "Wild Gratitude," in *Wild Gratitude* (New York: Alfred A. Knopf, 2003), p. 17.

4. I prefer the translation and compilation of Luke 6:20-21, Matthew 5:3-6, and Gospel of Thomas 54 and 69 in Guy Davenport and Benjamin Urrutia, *The Logia of Yeshua* (Washington, D.C.: Counterpoint, 1996), p. 4.

5. Cited in Dorothy Millar, *Seeds for the Morrow.*

6. John Dominic Crossan, *The Historical Jesus* (San Francisco: Harper San Francisco, 1991), pp. 225-348.

7. Gerhard Kittel, *Theological Dictionary of the New Testament* (Grand Rapids: Wm. B. Eerdmans, 1967), pp. 917-23.

8. Reinhold Niebuhr, *Justice and Mercy* (New York: Harper & Row, 1974), p. 15.

5. THE GETHSEMANE PRAYER: THY WILL BE DONE

1. Raymond Edward Brown, *The Death of the Messiah* (New York: Doubleday, 1994), 1:153.

2. James Hillman, *The Soul's Code: In Search of Character and Calling* (New York: Random House, 1996), p. 203.

6. PRAYERS FROM THE CROSS

1. In addition to the three prayers, the other four words were: (1) "I thirst," Jesus' identification with the human thirst for water and for God; (2) "Woman, behold your son; . . . [Son] behold your mother" (John 19:26-27), an act which gave his mother to the beloved disciple and the beloved disciple to his mother in ongoing relationship; (3) "Truly, I say to you, today you will dwell with me in paradise" (Luke 23:43), the gift of salvation to the thief on the cross beside him; (4) "It is finished," a declaration of the end and the completion of his life and mission.

2. Flannery O'Connor, cited in Andre Dubus, *The Times Are Never So Bad* (Boston: David R. Godine, 1983), frontispiece.

3. See photograph on the next page.

4. This story was told to me by Frye Gaillard from an interview he had with Lewis as part of a book Gaillard is writing on the Civil Rights movement in Alabama.

5. James W. Fowler, *Becoming Adult, Becoming Christian* (San Francisco: Harper & Row, 1984), pp. 121-22.

6. The rest of John 12:24 reads, ". . . it remains alone; but if it dies, it bears much fruit."

7. Peter Kreeft, *Making Sense Out of Suffering* (Ann Arbor: Servant Books, 1986), pp. 133-34.

8. Reinhold Niebuhr, *Justice and Mercy* (New York: Harper & Row, 1974), frontispiece.

7. PRAYERS FROM JOHN: THAT WE MAY BE ONE

1. In the notes of the introduction, I delineated three levels of historical remembrance reflected in the sayings of Jesus:

(1) Accurate historical memory of Jesus' actual words passed along in oral transmission, then translated into Greek; (2) A capturing of the ideas of Jesus in paraphrased form; or (3) the words the early church heard the Living Christ speaking to them through the Spirit, words which adapted and extended the meaning of Jesus' message for the situation of the church. John's Gospel is most possibly the latest of the four Gospels, written in the last decade of the first century, sixty or seventy years after Jesus. Its collection of the sayings of Jesus comes more from the third of these layers than from the first two, and more from the second than the first.

2. Dietrich Bonhoeffer, *Letters and Papers from Prison*, ed. Eberhard Bethge (London: SCM Press, 1953), p. 165.

3. See Raymond E. Brown, "The Gospel According to John," *Anchor Bible Dictionary*, vol. 29A (Garden City, N.Y.: Doubleday, 1966), p. 370.

4. Ibid., pp. 436-37.

5. See *Anchor Bible Dictionary*, 2:744.

6. Thomas Merton, *Conjectures of a Guilty Bystander* (Garden City, N.Y.: Doubleday, 1966), pp. 156-57.

7. As cited in Margaret Visser, *The Geometry of Love* (Toronto: HarperFlamingo, 2000), p. 18.

8. William James, *The Varieties of Religious Experience* (New York: The Modern Library, 1902), pp. 163-256.

9. Flannery O'Connor, *The Habit of Being: Letters of Flannery O'Connor* (New York: Farrar, Straus, Giroux, 1979), pp. 354-55.

10. Andrew Newberg and Eugene D'Aquili, *Why God Won't Go Away: Brain Science and the Biology of Belief* (New York: Ballantine Books, 2001).

11. See J. Louis Martyn, "Galatians," *The Anchor Bible Dictionary* (New York: Doubleday, 1997) for a brilliant new exposition of the "apocalyptic" message of Paul centering in the "new creation" as God's transforming invasion of the present age; also, his Shaffer Lectures at Yale University Divinity School in 2000.

12. Joseph Campbell, *The Power of Myth* (New York: Doubleday, 1988), pp. 8, 50.

13. Parker J. Palmer, *The Active Life: A Spirituality of Work, Creativity, and Caring* (San Francisco: Harper & Row, 1990), p. 8.

EPILOGUE: THE RISEN CHRIST RETURNS TO BLESS

1. *The Oxford Book of Prayer*, ed. George Appleton (New York: Oxford University Press, 1985), p. 205.

2. John P. Meier, *A Marginal Jew: Companions and Competitors* (New York: Doubleday, 2001), 3:20-21.

3. Mary Magdalene was called "apostle to the apostles" as early as the third century by Hippolytus, who named her *apostola apostolorum.*

4. Anne Lamott, *Traveling Mercies* (New York: Pantheon Books, 1999), p. 50.

5. Quoted from Anne Lamott's salon.com column, "A Spiritual Chemotherapy," Feb., 1997, p. 3.

6. Ibid., p. 4.

7. *Traveling Mercies*, p. 50.

A Guide for Small Groups

Kenneth H. Carter, Jr.

S tephen Shoemaker offers readers an opportunity to reflect on a subject that may be very much a part of our spiritual life—the Lord's Prayer. And yet many of us do not fully grasp the meanings or implications of these words. A study of this prayer and other prayers of Jesus will help us not only at an intellectual level, but also in our corporate and private practices of worship and devotion.

It will be helpful to meditate on this material in the context of a small group. After all, these words were given to the disciples who had prompted the teaching with the words, "Lord, teach us to pray" (Luke 11:2 NRSV). In other words, the prayer was intended for disciples living in community. The small group may take the form of a Sunday school class, a worship committee, an Emmaus Reunion group, a Covenant Discipleship group, a Women's Circle, or an early morning Bible Study. Any group that is grounded in the Christian experience would benefit from Shoemaker's reflections on the Lord's Prayer, words that are often spoken but not always reflected upon.

LEADING A SMALL GROUP

A small group focusing on *Finding Jesus in His Prayers* will need a leader or convener. As a convener, you will have the following responsibilities:

- Invite participants into the group experience.

- Interpret the study as an attempt to gain a greater appreciation of an essential, but often neglected, subject.

- Establish a group climate of support and accountability. Reassure participants that their experiences will be honored in the group—but also challenge them to consider perspectives that might be new or different to them.

The following guidelines might also help in the calling together of the group:

- Seek out individuals who are united by a common interest in the faith, but differ in their expressions of it. Think of individuals who do not naturally pray together, study together, serve together, or even worship together. A diversity of participants will enrich the experience of the group meetings.

- Establish an atmosphere of trust and acceptance. Prayer is an intimate and holy experience, and individuals will deepen in this practice as they come to trust God and one another. This takes time, and specific guidance from the convener.

- The development of a secure and even confidential community will enhance the willingness of participants to share their experiences of prayer, to bear one another's burdens, and to acknowledge their needs to forgive and be forgiven, to trust in God's providence of daily bread, and so on.

You might want to draft a simple covenant that will guide the group's experience in the coming sessions. The covenant might touch on the following matters:

- A willingness to listen attentively to others when not speaking

- A commitment to keep the discussion that is shared in the group confidential

- A decision to make attendance at the gatherings a priority in the participants' time schedule

- A receptivity to learning new ways of prayer, and more about prayer, as the words of Jesus take on new meanings.

THE ORGANIZATION OF THE LESSONS

The following format will allow the group to meet together in four sessions. The sessions may be once a week for four weeks. The advantage of this pattern is that individuals have time to reflect on the material over a period of several days. You might also consider adapting *Finding Jesus in His Prayers* into a retreat format, with the four meetings taking place on Friday evening, Saturday morning, Saturday afternoon, and Saturday evening. Whichever format is chosen, it is important not to race through the material. Instead, allow Stephen Shoemaker and the voices of Scripture and tradition to speak, and give ample time for silence, as God responds to our petitions.

If the study occurs over several weeks, have participants read the prologue, the introduction, and chapter 1 prior to the first meeting. If the study takes place over a weekend, encourage participants to read the material prior to the gathering.

THE FIRST MEETING

Introducing the Lord's Prayer

Begin by allowing the participants to introduce themselves. Ask them to open their copy of *Finding Jesus in His Prayers* to page 11, and say the words of the Lord's Prayer together.

- In the first meeting, participants will cover the prologue, the introduction, and chapter 1. Ask individuals to read through the prayers of Jesus (pages 11-13). Which are most familiar? Most surprising? Most difficult? Most comforting?

- "The Story of Jesus" is a brief narrative of the life of Jesus. It will help the leader to place the prayers in their contexts.

- The introduction sets the stage for the entire book. Shoemaker insists that the prayers of Jesus "reveal the spiritual core of his life with God," and that prayer is "primary speech." What does he mean by these statements? See page 17.

- On page 18, the author gives a critique of the "prayer of Jabez," contrasting a brief four-line prayer with nine prayers of the Lord that occur throughout the Gospels. Do you agree? Disagree?

- The excursus on the use of the word *Abba* is especially important, and will spark interest among participants (pages 21-23).

- How does the author contrast the importance of historical questions surrounding the prayers and their present meanings? What does it mean to "stand before" (page 25) one of these prayers?

- Chapter 1 places the prayers of Jesus within their Jewish contexts. Read the material related to morning, afternoon, and evening prayers. Ask the participants to share important practices or experiences of prayer at these times. The Jewish ritual for prayers of blessing before and after meals is also given. Someone in the group may also share a family tradition or discipline related to these occasions.

- On page 26, the author notes that Jesus prayed within the worshiping community and apart from it. Ask individuals within the group to reflect on the importance and uniqueness of each kind of prayer. What would be the danger of limiting ourselves to one form of prayer, either corporate or individual, to the exclusion of the others?

• On page 28, Shoemaker identifies three obstacles to authentic prayer, taken from Jesus' teaching in Luke 11: "no show-offy prayers, no long-winded prayers, no embarrassed prayers."

• Can anyone in the group recall a "show-offy prayer," an example of religious speech that was more for the benefit of a crowd than for God?

• Jesus critiques prayer that is "long-winded." Why, according to Shoemaker, does Jesus forbid this kind of prayer? (See pages 28-29.)

• How does the author connect a sense of shame and unworthiness with our lack of prayer? (See pages 29-30.)

• Finally, give a brief summary of the traditions of the words "debts," "trespasses," and "sins" in the Lord's Prayer.

• In closing, ask the participants to turn to pages 34-35, and say together the words from the ecumenical version of the Lord's Prayer.

THE SECOND MEETING

The Lord's Prayer

• Begin with a reading of the Lord's Prayer, using "trespasses" at the appropriate place. Ask participants to share any insights or lingering questions from the first meeting.

A Guide for Small Groups

• Discuss the shape of the prayer suggested by the author: a beginning, an ending, and two sets of petitions—one set of three petitions about God, another set of three petitions about us. Shoemaker notes the comment of Tertullian, early church teacher, that the prayer contains "a summary of the gospel." Read the divisions of the prayer again, from pages 35-36. Do you see it as a summary?

• Ask a member of the group to read the paragraph at the bottom of page 36, which is a reference to the use of the word *Abba*. Why is this distinction important? The author notes that the word *Abba* conveys both "intimacy and respect" (page 37). Why are both important and necessary?

• Reflect on the discussion of the word "our" preceding Abba. The author writes: "We pray *Abba* as a part of a community and members together of God's whole creation. The kingdom of God is not just personal; it is social and communal. 'Our *Abba*' better represents the character of the whole prayer" (page 38).

• What is the significance of prayer to "Our *Abba* in heaven"? See page 38.

• The first petition has to do with the hallowing of God's name. The author reflects on the importance of biblical names for God, the premodern meanings of naming someone, and the relation between prayer and magic (pages 39-41).

• What does it mean, according to Shoemaker, to hallow God's name? See pages 40-41 for two answers. Would individuals in the group offer additional meanings? The first meaning given by the author has to do with reverence and worship, the second to do with action and mission. Which is more a part of your understanding?

- Chapter 3 focuses on the remainder of the Lord's Prayer, beginning with the petition "Your kingdom come." Ask participants to read over pages 43-45. How would the group begin to define the kingdom of God? And is this necessary, if we are to know what we are praying about?

- The petition "Your will be done" is closely related to the prayer for the kingdom. What does the phrase "God's will" mean to members of the group? What insights does the author offer to this question?

- We pray for "daily bread." How is this petition both personal and corporate?

- In the author's reflection on the petition related to "forgiveness," he speaks of a "circle of conditionality" (page 50). Say the petition out loud. What is meant by the author's phrase? Is the image of the double-hinged door, swinging in and out, helpful to the group?

- In the reflection on temptation and evil, the author notes the experience of Jesus in Luke 4:1-13. Ask a member of the group to read this passage. What are our own temptations? How are we in need of protection?

- The chapter concludes with a moving account of a community's linking prayer and life. Read the experience in the group (pages 54-55), and conclude in silent prayer, before God in reverence and thanksgiving.

THE THIRD MEETING

Reversals, Gethsemane, Cross

- The fourth chapter begins with a meditation on praise and thanksgiving. Ask individuals to offer testimonies about the presence of God in their own lives and in the world. As a corporate response, read together the prayer on page 57.

• How is the praise of God present in the prayers of Jesus? In his life? See pages 57-61.

• The model of Jesus for us is to "give thanks amid the ruins" (page 62). How was this so in the life of Jesus? How is this so in our lives?

• Can you recall a time when you prayed through an experience of great difficulty? Take two or three minutes to silently reflect or recall that experience, or to journal about it.

• Can you recall a time in your life when God reversed your expectations? Ask a member of the group to say the prayer at the bottom of page 58.

• Go over the context for the prayer at Gethsemane (page 61).

• How is this a prayer about God's freedom and ours? See page 67. How is the prayer in the garden of Gethsemane related to the petitions of the Lord's Prayer, "Your kingdom come, your will be done"?

• How is the prayer at Gethsemane a part of our "primary speech"? How are we being asked to "watch and pray"?

• The author turns in chapter 6 to the prayers offered by Jesus from the cross. "As we face the worst that life can offer— terrorists flying aircraft into the World Trade Towers, betrayal at the hands of ones we trusted most, a disease which brings our life to a close—these prayers bring us what we need most." Ask the participants to read the words from the cross in preparation for the fourth and final group meeting. Conclude with a saying of the Lord's Prayer, using the word "debts" at the appropriate place.

THE FOURTH MEETING

Cross, Unity, Resurrection

• Begin with a reading of the Lord's Prayer, using the word "sins" at the appropriate place.

• We begin with Jesus' words of forgiveness from the cross. The author writes: "Jesus' prayer on the cross was the beginning of a forgiveness movement that has reached around the world; two thousand years later it is still at work healing the deepest wounds of humanity" (page 72). How is forgiveness a reality in our world today?

• On the cross, Jesus voices his sense of abandonment (quoting Psalm 22:1). Ask participants to reflect on times in their lives when they felt far from God. It is, the author insists, "the profoundest of pain, both psychologically and spiritually." And yet, in our distance from God and abandonment, Jesus has been there first, and is there for us, and with us.

• Jesus offers a model to us of relinquishment: *"Abba,* into thy hands I commit my spirit!" How are we called to relinquish? How are our lives offerings? How might we say these words as we prepare for sleep in the evening?

• Chapter 7 focuses on Jesus' prayers in the Gospel of John. Ask a member of the group to say the words from the prayer on pages 83-84.

• The author notes three prayers of Jesus in the Gospel of John. The first, John 12:27, echoes the prayer at Gethsemane. The second is his prayer at the tomb of Lazarus (John 11:41). The third is the primary focus of the chapter. It is the "high priestly prayer" of John 17, and it is a prayer for unity.

• Reflect on the unity described by Jesus in this prayer: "*Abba* and Jesus, Jesus and his disciples." This unity is relation, and is a oneness of "being," "moral purpose," and "mutual indwelling" (page 89). What do these terms mean and why are they important in understanding the prayer of Jesus?

• The author writes, "the oneness for which Jesus prayed on our behalf was the overcoming of the separateness or estrangement we feel in relation to God, self, others, and life itself" (page 91). Ask if any of the participants would like to speak of this yearning for unity.

• Discuss the distinction between "once-born" and "twice-born" individuals (pages 91-92). How does this fit with the experiences of group members?

• What characterizes a right relationship with God? With others?

• The epilogue gives an image of the risen Lord who comes to bless us and breathe life into us (see John 20). The Lord's Prayer can be as close to us, and as important, as our breathing. Invite group members to breathe deeply, symbolic of the Spirit's presence within them. Join hands and conclude with a saying of the Lord's Prayer, printed on pages 98-99.

• As the study concludes, invite participants to share the peace of the Lord with one another.